When the Honeymoon is Over

Patricia McElhone

When the Honeymoon is Over

Seven True Accounts of the
Experience of Marriage

Veritas Publications Dublin 1977

First published 1977 by
Veritas Publications,
Lower Abbey Street, Dublin 1.

Set in 11/12 Baskerville and
printed and bound in the Republic of Ireland by
Cahill (1976) Limited, Dublin.

Designed by Liam Miller.
Cover by Steven Hope.

Nihil Obstat:
Richard Sherry, DD.

Imprimi Potest:
✠Dermot,
Archbishop of Dublin.
April 13, 1977.

ISBN 0-905092-27-9.
CAT. NO. 3351.

Contents

1 Myself: the pain of loss

Did I know you at all? I wondered. The face, cold and handsome, could have been chiselled out of marble. The lips straight, neat, uncompromising. The closed lids, blank. Worst of all, the folded hands, fingers entwining the brown Rosary beads. Still fingers. Everywhere stillness. The phoney elegance of pleated white satin. Dear God, where was my man?

Someone pushed a chair behind my knees. It was better then. I could not see the whole, long, stiff form. Only the face, and here there was the suggestion of quiet laughter.

A street lamp turning his eyes to sea-green. Jealous eyes, I told him. Glad I was then, that it was for me they sparkled. Greed, mischief, impatience, shot streaks of light into the darkness of the car. Every "goodnight" under the street lamp was quick, high heels cracking off the pavements in the quiet, like caps shot out of a child's gun. Lifting the weatherboard on our front door, so that it would not drag along the stone doorstep. The car cruising quietly away, out of gear.

Weeks of exploring, for him the excitement of comparison. For me the first dawning of love, permanence. Always the feeling that bondage, even tyranny, was never too far removed.

Clashes of temperament. For me feeble attempts to shrug off the magnetism of this green-eyed, determined lover. He, too, shrugging off the idea of permanence. Parting after weekends spent walking, driving, or just sitting. Always somewhere near the sea.

How we both loved the sea. The restless, furious force that could also spread out in great calm and beauty. Like our own unruly emotions, sweeping and swamping. Never just standing still. When the sun shone across an evening tide, touching every little swell that crept on to the shingle at our feet, our souls were drowning too. In the stillness, often in silence, there grew the recognition of soul mates, differing, yet fusing at some unknown level.

At last, decision. Breaking it off. Some age difference making him reluctant to take on a raw, high-spirited girl.

Difference, too, in upbringing. He, the oldest son of a widowed mother, had started work on the street where I was born, the year that I was born. He, a newly fledged teenager, assuming the role of father to his orphaned brothers. I, growing up under his eyes, totally unaware that fathers die, mothers weep, children suffer and are sad.

On our street, we all loved this gay, generous lad. Paying the bread bill for our mother, we would never come away empty-handed. I'll always taste those fresh Chester cakes. Bagging the job of paying that bill had to be arranged well in advance. We all wanted it.

The years in between, while I went to school, loving it, no longer interested in Chester cakes.

He, too, wending his way to success in business.

I, leaving school, realising the dream of my girlhood years. I entered a convent.

Not really attracted to the life as such, but quite sure that God wished this from me. Farewell parties, dancing, always dancing. And then I went. My mother always thought I was making a mistake. How I must have hurt her, with my youthful omniscience.

To this day, I never know which of us made the mistake. In my diary, some three years later, I find this entry: "Today, I left the convent": five words written on a single page, like so many stunted bushes in a frosted field. The bleak desolation blows wanly now, across the years.

For when, one day, I crossed the threshold of my chosen convent, I walked with tear-streaked joy. Leaving home was bitter grief. I went alone. But underlying was the peace of generous giving. Eager hands stretched out to help, and convent life soon claimed each waking hour.

Problems there were, in plenty, but faith and hope attended each new tomorrow.

As months lengthened, convent life was graven,

not in shallow wanderings, but in deep renunciations. No stone enclosure seals off the outside world more surely than detachment's warm abandon.

And then the first cold feel of weakening flesh, gladly borne as yet another trial. More days and weeks and months, until the sentence was pronounced, not mine the way of chaste perfection.

Unquestioning obedience stilled the fear of numberless tomorrows, adrift in wastes of barren, cold indifference. No comfort now in Mother Superior's wise serenity. Cool eyes dismissed the misery of young uncertainty.

And so these words were penned that now unleash the floods of desolation, bringing to mind the city railway station, teeming crowd, the solitary figure unused to shorter garb and ugly hair, cowering at the memory of frigid farewell, dreading the prospect of unsure welcome.

Returning, as I had left, alone. But no peace for the generous giving now — only confusion, hurt and doubtful physical health.

My mother welcomed me back, not sure what was to become of me but putting a brave face on her fears and disappointments.

My father, quietly glad to have his "singing-bird" near him again.

For me, here, the first experience of real sorrow. My older sister had died suddenly, aged twenty-two, while I lay ill on the other side of Ireland. Our bedroom was haunted with echoes of girlhood secrets, whispered in those hours before sleep comes, when confidences shelter in the dusk.

Her place was empty, and so too was my life, until youth, security, good friends and the healing of time touched those lonely places and they were gone.

Lonely again, now, several years later, when this man who had awakened me to a new love, held back, as yet unsure. He had so much to give up, for what must have seemed so little.

Misery. No one, among my many friends, who could take his place. Dancing dates for me, who still loved to dance the nights away. Restlessness for him, who never danced, but who now found he could not shut out the memory of this ridiculous intruder into his round of race-meeting, dog-coursing, story-telling men friends, with knowing eyes and jibing tongues.

Emptiness for me in shallow youth. Unquiet, like sleeping on a bad bed. Tossing about to find a real resting place.

And then, surrender. Uncertain on so many levels. Dead sure, somewhere in the depths. An act of faith, a jump in the dark.

For me, the comfort of a real man who had lived, worked and loved, and who still wanted me more than any of these.

For him, the possession of a potential woman, loving, undisciplined, entirely undomesticated.

Never too much discussion about the future, just a crumbling before something bigger than both of us.

A wedding, no bells. Rain and a cold, early morning church, quite deserted except for the vital four, the priest, and perhaps, I cannot quite remember, an early morning Mass goer.

One vivid recollection here, of stumbling on the words "I plight thee my troth". An anxious look and then, a big, warm hand closing around my small, cold fingers. In all the years I can remember the comfort of that hand. I still feel the trust that flowed between us at that moment.

Cars, trains, a plane, a taxi, a huge hotel. A lift whirring up to room 504.

Strangers, strangeness, everything hazy. An evening meal in a dining room as big as the railway station at home. A frigid, condescending head-waiter. A walk in the London streets, locating a newsagency, making sure of an Irish morning paper.

At last, it could not be delayed any longer. Bed-time. Two beds, a private bathroom where he disappeared to undress. I making sure that I would be in my bed before he came back, wearing the prettiest nightie I had ever possessed, worrying that I would disappoint him, that my figure was not all that wonderful, that he would find me wanting in so many ways. I remember praying, and thinking of my mother.

And then he came, looking very unfamiliar.

The strongest feeling I had that night was fear. I wondered how much I knew this man — did I know him at all? He was kind, patient. I, passive, detached, anxious.

Honeymoon over, back to a cottage home. An alarm clock breaking the day for us at six a.m. on a Monday.

He starting out to his week's work. I, left behind in the emptiness. Cases unpacked. Dirty clothes to be washed. Could it be I who would have to scrub the shirt collars, wash the hankies?

How quiet it all was, and lonely. My mother, strictly adhering to custom, denied me a visit home until I would be one month married.

My husband, anxious to form my character, decided not to ring or write before his return on Friday.

All week I practised cooking fish. I scorched the white shirt fronts with an over-hot iron. I cried with frustration when rinse after rinse failed to take off the brown marks.

Friday came. I remember little, except a sorry looking piece of fish.

And so we were launched, very much in a minor key.

Not for long, though. One evening I sat down on the floor, leaning against his knees, and told him we were expecting a baby.

A vivid memory here. Very little said. For him a great, quiet joy in the softening of his eyes, a glowing love, concern and pride.

For me, the beginning of many miseries. Sickness. Hair gone lank and dull. Legs disfigured by ugly veins. Away with the shiny, high-heeled shoes.

Learning to feed a man, when every smell of food sent me heaving to the sink.

Miseries soon forgotten. Another diary entry:

Wednesday 25 May, our first child was born.

At six a.m. the gravel path to our cottage door was silvered by the morning sun. In our gable field, a cuckoo called. The wooden gate creaked under the doctor's hand. Our small room was busy for an hour and then the day was ours. Dad's and mine, with our new son.

This baby giving me back my vitality, the shine to my hair, a glow to my skin.

Giving my husband a new woman to hold, lovingly. Giving him something wonderful to come home to, and very soon deposing the dogs, the horses and the short drinks.

More sons and daughters. Great joy in their arrivals. Several house moves. Problems. Sickness.

Two weeks after our fifth child was born, my husband was taken to hospital. I will never forget the misery. He was never a letter writer, indeed the only letters he ever wrote to me were from hospital.

These pencilled words still jump to life every time I read this precious letter. He wrote as he spoke, bluntly. Seemingly casual, and it still scalds my heart across the twenty years.

We had been to visit him and the letter began:

What a thrill and a shock to see you and the love parade on Tuesday. I was very proud of ye all; they all looked so well. Your face comes before me very much and you are still streets ahead of anyone we have here. So you are still No. 1 and will always be.

And so it was. Underneath all the problems there was content.

For me a developing maturity. For him, complete engrossment in his family unit. Always generous, still presenting a tough exterior.

Another vivid memory here, across twenty-one years.

It was winter and dark outside the windows. There was a bright fire in the grate and I was feeding our second child. The older boy, of about thirteen months, was propped up among the cushions of a deep, comfortable couch. It was about tea-time and suddenly, Dada appeared beyond the uncurtained window. It was very cold and his face was red from the wind. Shading his eyes with one hand he looked in at us there, his care and his love. Tenderness softened his face. Putting a heavy cushion in front of the older child, I went to the door carrying the baby. To this day I can hear my husband say "Every picture tells a story": we were together, we were happy, we were all his, just waiting for his return home.

Even when our first child was still in his pram, he used to lean forward to watch the car leaving on a Monday morning. This child had very beautiful eyes and he would turn to me lifting up his baby arms and, having in his eyes a lost look, he would say "Dada all gone". His small hands would flop down again, his lips droop and the house would almost sigh with the child.

Small children growing up. Eventually grown up. Still a little one left, though. Years passing. Growing conflicts as each child develops his own personality. Always a homely feeling about the house. Everyone having the habit of pushing in the front or back door and calling out "Mum, where are you?" Where was I? — always there.

No tyranny here. The years just seeming to roll gently by, full of children and care of the house, the latter very much a minority interest.

There were highlights, like the birth of our first daughter after three sons. For my husband, who had no sister, almost a miracle. This little girl child winding herself round his heart, the boys suffering a few emotional bruises until Father adjusted to his little girl.

In my diary I noted that on a snowy, bitterly cold morning, by candle and fire light, our first daughter was born:

> Every light in the house had gone out, so that I could not see very well the tiny, premature baby. No washing, no clothing this scrap of girlhood. The doctor, very gentle, saying: "Perhaps God has just lent you this little one for a very short while." Dad coming home from his week's journey did not seem too upset by her tiny body. He just willed her to stay alive.

For two weeks we had to employ a boy to carry turf in from an outhouse, up a long flight of stairs, to stack it outside my bedroom door so that the fire could be kept going night and day. I was kept in bed because of complications after my third child. My mother and father held the fort downstairs with the other three children. A nurse called each day to rub warm oil on the tiny baby. A wonderful woman doctor would sit in front of the fire, with a pipette, trying to drop some nourishment under the baby's tongue. She could neither suck, nor cry.

For six weeks the household scarcely breathed; my bedroom was the centre of hope and worry and love. I can remember the aching, tedious hours I spent trying to nourish this child, and then, the triumph of seeing her tiny jaws contract for the first time.

My friends collected dolls' clothes so that when the time came to discard the gamgee jacket and dress this little scrap we had garments small enough. The priest came to the house to administer baptism. I held the baby in my arms. No one in that room ever thought the baby would survive, except her father and myself. We prayed and often I cried.

The evening our first boy went to boarding school, I shall always remember. Suffering for him and for me. Again, his father was away from home, as his work demanded. This parting was like hacking a piece out of my own body. In my diary, Thursday 3 September:

Tom went to school. A sharp and brilliant autumn morning, with the wistful poignance of dying summer days smiting our hearts. Round the breakfast table a careful casualness, the younger ones sensing the significance of packed suitcases and unfamiliar, formal clothes. The smell of frying rashers and freshly brewed tea,

the unheard of courtesies of handing down to
Tom the marmalade and the treasured crispy
rasher rinds. The countless snares that might
unman this tall youngster. And then the hours
had flown, until the tea table was cleared and
the suitcases hoisted to check once more the
items, only this time an odd packet of sweets
was tucked into a folded sock top, a shirt sleeve
or a pyjama pocket. The children clustered
round the porch, cases being put into the car,
the stinging of unshed tears, the anguish of a
first-born's first parting. Saying goodbye at the
college, a boy standing alone, making a half
gesture towards the customary goodnight kiss,
and drawing back, conscious of his new status.

I remember a vase of chrysanthemums to welcome me home from hospital, chosen and arranged
by my husband, who never before had done such a
thing. I thought those flowers should never die.

There were weekend walks and picnics. Father
always organising the food, burying the big, dark
bottles of milk in a damp part of the sandy beach,
with the neck out, so that the children would have
a cool drink. Sometimes he would arrange the
bottles in a stream.

The woods were favourite places. Children
loving the mystery of half dark hide outs, the soft-
ness of pine needles under their feet, the way the
sun patterned the ground wherever the leaves parted to let in the light.

I would listen to the birds or the bubbling
streams running among the ferns. There was great

peace in the woods, the children's shouting seemed to dissolve into the great heights of the trees. Father would prop himself against some sturdy stump and read the Sunday papers.

Years of ordinary family life. Noise and fun. Crying and worrying, but a basic, secure affection.

Weekends now are unbearably empty. No small children, no picnics, no Father.

When holiday weekends come round, and the family disperses to play golf, go walking, or sometimes watch television, I go to bed and in the curtained room try to shut out the busy sounds of cars, voices and laughter.

Looking back now, it seems as if the personal relationship that began on the night we went out on our first date, was somehow suspended for about twenty years.

I cannot honestly recall blissful nights. There were the children of course. Always a cot in the bedroom, or a Moses basket. Always trying not to disturb the sleeping children. Having a husband away for five nights a week took a large slice out of our lives together.

But the years had changed us too. I, no longer the uncertain, anxious bride. Now knowing that I had not fallen short of my husband's expectations. Had far exceeded them, perhaps.

I knew I was his life, his great joy. He was demanding, yes. Possessive, yes. But with a great, generous spirit.

He, by nature an organiser. I fitting into each situation as he arranged it.

Eventually, we became so close as to almost think together, even when we were physically separated. Whatever upset him worried me too. If I became very tired, as I often did, he fussed over me like a mother hen.

Our love was seldom spoken of. I cannot ever remember saying "I love you". Indeed, I could not.

Nor did he speak of his love for me. I think perhaps he would have liked to, but I always thought our love was so personal, so very precious, that to try and label it would somehow reduce it to the ordinary, where it just did not belong.

Our physical expression of this love became something very precious and wonderful. That day when I sat in the mortuary, watching his stiff hands, I could feel them on my body, warm, strong and passionate.

For him, and from him, I had learned to express myself, wordlessly, because there just weren't words big enough or deep enough.

His death was gradual. He lost his vigour, his independence. His leg was amputated. The frustrations of this were terrible to watch. Fighting every inch of the way, he refused to give in. From his downstairs bed he ruled us all. He planned for the future.

The day our youngest little girl received her first holy communion, she stood in front of her Daddy, turning round to show him the dainty, puffed out skirt, the graceful veil, the sparkling little face full of excitement and joy. He sat there and watched the two of us leave his room. A bitter moment here; for us the special occasion, the assurance of nice clothes but most of all the use of our legs to take us out into the lovely sunshine, away from him.

Later that day, when we had settled him into the car to drive into the country, he would not let us take off our finery. With great reluctance he agreed to let me take off my big, white picture hat.

That same hat next came out of the box when Dad was already ten months dead and I was inside the sanctuary of our cathedral, with all my children, watching our oldest boy being ordained to the priesthood.

This day, too, I will never forget. Looking back on it now, another year later, it seems as if someone else was inside my flowered frock that day for surely my heart was somewhere among the spirits of the dead. This other me spoke and moved, ate and was photographed in the big white hat. There was again glorious sunshine, exultant organ music, excitement and joy. All through the ceremony, my little girl swung her legs, out and in, out and in, her white knee stockings and shoes catching the sunlight pouring in through the beautiful, stained glass windows.

There was a bleakness in my heart that stiffened my face into some semblance of composure. Perhaps it was for this day my love and I had been born, wed and parted.

We had suffered too. I remember the night before my husband went to Dublin for his amputation. His foot was gangrenous and climbing the stairs was agony. I was just behind him on the way up when it struck me it could be the last time we would ever go to bed together again. When I had helped him to undress, got the sore foot settled under a frame and tucked him in for the night, he was almost asleep from exhaustion. By the time I got in beside him, he was too tired to notice that I was kissing him goodnight.

What an ending to the glorious years.

There was pain, sordid physical deterioration, and still my man's full determination to survive and ignore the indications.

I, a woman, fully aware of my own desires, deeply conscious of his frustrations.

I, accepting that his life was almost over, leaving me on the lonely summit, on to which our love had swept us.

It was there he left me, suddenly, one day.

I always knew the bed we shared would be the emptiest corner of my new widowhood. And so it is.

It is such a big bed, where our children were conceived and born, where they all loved to cuddle in out of a bad dream, and where they were always welcomed and comforted.

It was here we would chat quietly before we slept, or when we woke early.

It was here I had often wished to melt away, somewhere inside him, and be safe forever.

2 Gerry and Eilis

When I set out to meet Gerry and Eilis it was dark and wintry. The country road was brightened here and there by the lighted windows of scattered houses. The path to their front door was rough and stony. An outside light shone on the beginnings of a garden.

Inside it was warm. Gerry, thirty-one, snoozed by the fireside. A feeding bottle sat on the stone hob of a generous fireplace. A baby chair lay sideways on the floor.

Eilis, twenty-eight, rushed into the room ahead of me still wearing her coat. Thumping cushions, explaining how she'd been delayed at a meeting, she brought energy and liveliness into the room.

Gerry settling down to talk. Eilis leaning forward, elbows on knees, alert.

Just seventeen months married, with a baby son, this couple both come from farming backgrounds. Gerry, one of ten children, whose father died when he was eight years old. Eilis one of five girls.

They met originally at a dance, when both were doing other lines. Some years later they met again, when Eilis asked for and got a lift to Dubin. She was en route to Germany to spend Christmas with her boy-friend's family. Gerry was going to Dublin to meet his girl-friend. Chatting on the journey they discovered many similar interests, among them badminton. Back home after the holidays, Gerry rang Eilis and they arranged a game of badminton. And so it started.

Eilis was less interested in Gerry than he in her. The German line was broken and Eilis emerged tougher, wiser and extremely cautious. One of the greatest strains of her four years' German line had been deceit, so she resolved thereafter to be brutally frank about everything.

Gerry was attracted by her outspokenness. They discovered a great deal in common and both feel very strongly that the similarity of their backgrounds gave the relationship a significant stability.

Eighteen months passed in discovering what appeared like complete compatibility, enjoying one another's company, walking, dancing, watching films. Realising that being together was what made their happiness.

Both were tolerant of the idea of sex before marriage, without either having had this experience. Gerry saying that he never seemed to meet this kind of girl, and glad now that he hadn't. Admitted feeling envious of various room mates during student days who freely discussed the casual girl friends who were quite willing to go to bed.

For Gerry and Eilis their pre-marriage course was one of the happiest experiences of courtship, because of the chats and discussions after the talks. While welcoming the positive approach of the course, they were a bit surprised that no danger areas were mentioned. Preferring, however, the note of complete optimism. Feeling that their previous experience of doing long lines was their greatest asset. Also having complete freedom between them to air their honest opinions.

Merging finally, a temperamentally differing pair, but basically sharing one another's views about most things.

Eilis, quick to anger, and as quick to forget.

Gerry, very slow to lose his temper, but slow to forget words spoken in anger.

Deciding to start a family soon after marriage because Eilis had worries about her ability to conceive. Some years previously she'd had one of her ovaries removed and this bothered her enough after she was married to make her visit her gynaecologist. She now has a very welcome baby son.

Before they were married it was decided that Eilis would keep on working at her profession, and so she does. Her parents live near and they take the baby each morning, keeping him until her working day is finished in mid-afternoon.

Gerry agrees to all this. His only anxiety is that Eilis should become over-tired. She is brisk, capable and manages to keep well ahead of her household chores. She is quite determined not to become a full-time housewife, feels in fact that she would go "clean round the bend" if she had to stay about the house all day.

Both realise she's just not that kind of girl.

Gerry, for the first time, appreciates his own mother's hard life, keeping hens, working on a farm with a bad house and no water supply. He resolves to make life easier for his wife.

Eilis resents that her father took no share in household chores. She's anxious lest her husband should become completely reliant on her for meals and such.

They discuss the possibility of another, Eilis looking forward to another child, but no sooner than two years hence, at least.

Both talking this over.

Eilis just wondering which method of spacing their children will be most suitable for her. Rejecting the pill on medical grounds. Regarding the IUD (intra-uterine device) as unnatural, and utterly distrustful. Thinking the Billings method will probably be most suitable.

Gerry of the opinion that once fertilisation has taken place, no form of prevention or termination of pregnancy is moral. Quite willing to agree to whichever family planning method she decides on.

Both considering the possibility that there could be another pregnancy sooner than they might wish. Agreeing that they would simply have to accept this and make the best of it. She more grudgingly than he.

Love? For Gerry, concern for his wife's happiness the most important thing in his life. He realises that her worry is his and her distress or discomfort, his. Tells her often that he loves her. Feels quite sure that so many shared interests between them guarantee happiness and a good partnership. He foresees no problem that could not be discussed and settled between them. He thinks that sexual compatibility makes their relationship completely harmonious.

Eilis wonders at how her love has deepened in marriage and feels she loves him more than she had thought possible. She finds herself much more affected by her husband's attitude to everything now, than before she was married. She realises that she approached marriage coldly, determined to make a succes of it, as she would any other project she was involved in. Now she finds herself totally absorbed, and feels very happy about this. Relies greatly on honesty between them. Does not feel there is much danger of direct confrontation about any issues, when they can talk things out between them.

Gerry and Eilis both apologise for not having had any rows so far, either in courtship or marriage. Again they compare this experience to their previous affairs, when both couples fought three-quarters of the time.

They feel that they've both been very busy this past eighteen months, getting a new house built, putting it into shape, having a baby, learning to cope. They realise, of course, that problems *will* come, but are quite sure that together they can handle anything that comes up.

For Eilis, God is important. Prayer, too. She thanks God for her husband, her baby, everything. Finds prayer difficult if she's down in the dumps about anything. Likes to feel she's on good terms with the Lord, worries about sin in marriage, whether or not this is possible, and if so, whether she has sinned. Feels anxious about enjoying sex up to a point, while still avoiding the possibility of becoming pregnant.

Wonders about all this and seems to rely on hearsay and gossip, having no positive information one way or another. Feels that while she was attending the pre-marriage course, one of its greatest attractions was the absence of "thou shalt nots"; now wondering if she would have preferred to have a complete understanding of what does and does not constitute a sin within marriage. Considerable anxiety and confusion here. Regretting that this anxiety, at the moment, prevents her from receiving the Eucharist.

Gerry has no particular worry about anything and certainly does not share this anxiety of his wife. Thinks now that his early training has left him with a judicial God. Has always feared punishment for wrongs done. Realising that in his youth he felt a decent life was his birthright, without reverting to God. The sudden death of a friend affected him deeply and brought him up against the uncertainty of life. This experience has brought him to suppliant prayer for his wife, his infant child, and his own life. He asks God to help him, thanks him for all the things he now enjoys. Always finds it hard to relate to the God figure of his youth, a God who is waiting to punish him.

Eilis and Gerry pray each evening, separately. Both feel they would like their son to grow up with faith in God, and would like to do all they can to foster this faith in their home.

Home is important to this couple. They are grateful for what they have. They have confidence in the future.

I left them with the same confidence. There is nothing starry-eyed in their attitude. They have determination, common sense and a very sane approach to life.

Love seems almost to have taken them by surprise, as if they had rationalised every aspect of their relationship before marriage and found afterwards, unexpectedly, this quality of caring. This they regard as treasure indeed.

3 Joe and Margaret

Joe and Margaret are five years married. They live in a new house set down in the middle of a row of old houses. There was street lighting. The houses were odd shapes and sizes. Some had small gardens. Others had front doors opening directly on to the street. Outside Joe's front door there hung an amber-shaded light. Inside there was a pram in the hall, quiet in the house and a good fire blazing in the sittingroom grate. And so we settled down to talk.

Joe left the National School at fifteen and started to work in a hotel. His next job was labouring, and he cycled six miles to and from work every day. He appreciated every penny he earned. He handed his wages to his mother, who was decent with him. She wasn't out to grab and gave him back what she considered fair.

Joe now has a decent job with a good wage. He is always aware of his good fortune in having his job, his car, his own home. He takes pride in his

ability to supply plenty of good, wholesome food
for the household. Whatever the disadvantages of
his early years, he is now a good-looking, intelli-
gent young man, with an easy manner. Neither he
nor Margaret takes a drink.

Margaret, who worked as a teacher up to her
marriage, has three sisters and one brother. Her
parents are alive. Margaret kept up her job until
the baby arrived. She is now a pretty woman,
quietly spoken and unhurried in her movements.
Joe is talkative and laughs often. While they both
talk there is evidence of complete harmony and if
there is a difference in their academic achievements,
there is no lack of balance in their attitudes to life.

Joe and Margaret met at a dance, the only
place one could meet in the West of Ireland of five
years ago, they say. They were immediately
attracted to one another. Joe liked Margaret's simplicity and especially her natural good looks without make-up. Margaret found she could talk easily
to Joe, and more important, there were worth-
while things to talk about, not the usual dancehall
banalities. Margaret had never done a line before,
while Joe had had a few short attachments. Neither
felt inclined to form or sustain an attachment without being seriously attracted.

They were going out together for a year and a
half before marriage. Neither attended a pre-
marriage course. Their dates were spent walking or
going to a film or play. Once they decided to get
married they spent months planning their home.
First they lived in a flat, and as they said "played

house" with drawing paper and pens, and household and do-it-yourself magazines. They both chose to live in a street rather than in a housing estate. They value the permanence of being securely established in an old part of the town and living among old residents.

Joe and Margaret are provident by nature. Their plans were so detailed that they knew what sort of flowers they wanted in their garden. They spent weeks walking around housing estates, antique and furniture shops. The success of their efforts is evident. Joe loves to sit in front of his sitting room fireplace and admire the stonework of the surround. He actually chose and picked the stones himself.

Where there was disagreement over any item, they talked it over and compromised. There were minor disagreements but never a row.

Before marriage they discussed money, their home and the possibility of having children. Both wanted children and agreed that if they did not have any of their own, they would adopt a child.

They have, in fact, an adopted son of eighteen months. They brought him home when he was two weeks old.

They talked about family planning before marriage, but made no hard-line decision at this stage. As it happened, the problem has not arisen.

When Margaret did not become pregnant, they both consulted a doctor and Margaret spent some time in the care of a gynaecologist. Both were quite happy to accept their failure to have their own baby and are overwhelmed by their love for their little adopted son. They plan a second adoption as soon as there is a baby available.

Should they still succeed in having a baby of their own, they would be grateful and happy. Both are aware that this could happen, and indeed that it does often happen, when a couple adopts a child. They are completely relaxed about these possibilities, and have confidence that in supplying unbounded love to their adopted children, they will be ensuring their own and the children's future happiness. Margaret laughingly says that their little boy cannot have any faults but her own and Joe's, because no one else has cared for the child since he was two weeks old.

When Joe and Margaret go out, Margaret's mother baby-sits.

Love is the overall atmosphere in this home. As Joe says, they often wonder how they considered their first love to be real love. The maturing of their love has seemed something of a miracle. For this they are grateful, and yet they are aware that some suffering could be the price of such love. Margaret could not imagine any greater disaster in her life than Joe's death. If he were ill she would still have him, so sickness would be tolerable.

Both Joe and Margaret agree that sex is very important in marriage, although a lot of other things are also important, such as compatibility and complete honesty with one another. They say, however, that sex *is* very important, and at the same time they feel that sex is over-emphasised in present-day propaganda. In this, as in all other matters discussed, Margaret and Joe are careful to avoid extravagance of expression. They have no problems with sex, no problems with anything else either for that matter.

Religion is very much part of their lives. They pray together and say the Rosary together every night, as they were accustomed to doing in their own homes. Sometimes they pray in the car if they are late coming home. They do a lot of driving in Joe's off time. They visit his brother who lives in a very isolated country house. They take the baby with them on their outings and often laugh about the extent of the little boy's travels so far.

Joe's priorities are life, health and peace in the home. Money is not very important. He says if he were promoted in his job and required to move out of his present house, he would refuse it. He has everything from life he ever dreamed of having and is content and grateful.

Margaret has no desire to continue her work, now that she has her son. She does not want to miss one second of his growing and is determined to involve herself fully with her children. She remembers, when she herself was young, feeling shattered if her mother was out of the house when she came in from school. It seldom did happen but the emptiness was terrible. There was just no one else who took the same interest in her day's doings.

Margaret feels that being a fulltime housewife has made her a much more complete member of the community. It gives her more leisure to chat to the neighbours when she meets them, whereas when she was working she did not even know the names of other people living in the street. Now she would know if one of them were ill or in trouble, and feels this is how she likes to be.

The loss of a second salary coming into the house is not a factor. They always lived on Joe's anyway, and used hers to buy things for the house. Now their house is furnished and they have everything in it that they set out to have.

They enjoy their outings together when they plan them. A staff function is their annual dress-up affair. Before he was married, and until their little boy arrived, Joe enjoyed going to football matches. They travelled to Dublin for the finals and stayed overnight. It was like a second honeymoon, Joe said.

Now one of their regular outings together is attending the Christian Family Movement meetings. They enjoy the discussions and find that a lot of helpful suggestions are pooled to the benefit of all, such things as "what to tell the children and when; how to help the children to pray and understand their religion". Man and wife relationships are discussed. Things that have been heard on radio or seen on tv relating to marriage, for example a write-in on silences in marriage, were discussed. Couples talk freely of their own experiences and problems. Margaret and Joe feel that they have learned a lot from other people whom they know to be in similar circumstances to their own. Not all the meetings are solemn. They enjoy a good laugh together now and then, and all-in-all are a happy, neighbourly group.

Margaret belongs to an Association of Apostolic Work, where members knit or sew for the missions. This involves a fortnightly meeting. Joe helps in a voluntary social centre once a fortnight. Joe admits that he loves to sit at home. He thoroughly enjoys reading the local and provincial newspapers. He says he just settles down with his papers and throws one to Margaret, hoping she'll keep quiet long enough for him to read. They have their favourite tv programmes but are not addicted.

Both Joe and Margaret are grateful for the good fortune that brought them together. They dread becoming selfish or self-centred. I do not think they need worry. There is serene maturity in this household. There is no desire to get on in the world, nor yet any evidence of an inferiority complex.

They are simple, secure people, with faith in God and one another. Maybe it seems too good to be true, but there is depth in this simplicity. Their own home backgrounds were secure in affection, but life was hard. There were no luxuries. Their present way of life is still not luxurious. It is comfortable.

Their care for other people should guard them from ever becoming selfish. The atmosphere in this house is like the glow of a good fire on a cold evening. It touches you with welcome and warmth and undoubtedly springs from the love between Joe, Margaret and their small son.

4 Mark, Mary and Anne

Mark is a tall, fine-looking man of forty-nine. He speaks softly and has the physique of a rugby player. There is laughter behind his eyes, but there is wistfulness too, and gentleness.

He was married for the first time at the age of twenty-seven. Mary, his bride, was twenty-six. They met at a dance, in a hotel where Mark and two men friends came every year for a golf week-end. They were immediately attracted to each other and met again in Dublin, where they both lived.

Mark worked as representative for a well-known firm. Mary was a fully qualified accountant, a rare enough profession for a woman in the 1950s. Mark's work took him into the provinces and their courtship was almost confined to correspondence. After three months they became engaged, and within two years they were married. During their engagement Mark travelled to Dublin once a month and they would go to a picture together, or a dance. During winter a supper dance on Friday night was their regular outing.

Neither Mark nor Mary attended a pre-marriage course, because in those days there was not such emphasis on this sort of preparation for marriage. Both wanted children and talked about it before they married, but once they discovered that they were both keen to have children, the matter was not discussed in any great depth.

It is understandable, perhaps, that the main issue between them was money. Mary was earning more than Mark and was, in fact, capable of keeping them both. Mary's employer suggested that Mark should seek indoor employment in his own firm, which would enable them both to live in Dublin and Mary to continue at her own work.

After much discussion, when Mark decided that he would never get on in his own sphere if he passed up the promotions which necessitated moving out of Dublin, they agreed that Mary would give up her work and move with him to the north-west. Mary was quite willing and it never appeared to crop up afterwards as a regret.

Mark's income was £500 a year, and so they set about dividing up their money into slots — for monthly rent, food, phone and saving. Actually they did save, mostly because they got a rented cottage, fully furnished, at £60 a year.

Mark is very emphatic that where possible a girl should have a certain fixed sum, however small, for her very own, which she may spend as she wishes and no questions asked. He thinks it is very

degrading for any girl, especially one who has been
used to a good salary of her own, to have to ask
her husband for the price of a pair of tights. And
so they allowed one another £5 a month each.

Life for Mary would seem to have been rustic,
tucked away in a remote country town. The
cottage they rented was owned by a retired colonel
of the Indian army, who himself lived nearby.
Mary was always a dog lover and their household
included two very large dogs. Exercising these dogs
was a part of her daily routine, and as most of the
other residents of the town seemed to be dog
lovers and retired British army personnel, an
immediate social contact was established.

Mark was away for some part of each week, so
Mary quickly settled in among her new friends.
Mark describes the set-up as snobbish, and laughs
as he remembers how he was included in weekend
parties as Mary's husband. Besides the dogs Mary
was keen on gardening, another shared interest
with her neighbours. Mark was a keen golfer and
Mary played, but not seriously. They had a boat
and enjoyed sailing together.

Evening walks together would end with a visit
to one or other of their friends for a cup of coffee.
Television was at this time a novelty and did not
interfere with people gathering for a yarn.

Both Mary and Mark were aware of the
necessity of working together for the success of
their marriage. For them the grace of the sacra-
ment was all-important. As Mark put it, they never
considered because they went into a church and

there were joined in Matrimony, that *ipso facto* their future happiness was assured. They were both deeply committed Christians, but not "holy" people. Prayer together was something they worked at. They tried to say the Rosary together in Lent and during October. In any trouble they prayed.

One day, while Mary was bending down to take ashes out of the grate, she hurt her back and for three years suffered constant pain and the discomfort of a plaster on her back. Already Mark and Mary had been to doctors and a gynaecologist to establish their ability to have children. Initially nothing was discovered, but ultimately a gynaecologist operated on Mary to correct a womb displacement. All the doctors maintained that there was no physical cause for their failure to have a child.

Mark was then moved to the south of Ireland. They decided to go to London to consult a surgeon about Mary's back. During this period both Mary and Mark formed an attachment to St Jude and prayed daily for his intercession on their behalf. After two visits to the London surgeon Mary was cured, and two very grateful people came home to Ireland.

One evening, while they were sitting on either side of the fireplace, Mary asked Mark if he remembered a visit they had made together to Farm Street church in London. He did remember. She told him she had promised that day that if her back was cured, she would adopt a baby. Mark was overjoyed because he, too, had made the same promise, both unaware of the other's intention. So there and then Mark went to the phone and contacted a priest who, he knew, was interested in placing homeless children. It so happened that a baby girl, born in England to an Irish mother, was available for immediate adoption, so once more Mark and Mary took off and returned home with their six-weeks-old baby daughter. At this stage they had been married six years. A few years later they adopted a boy, travelling to England as before.

Soon after their little girl arrived, Mary had a visit one day from a rather grand lady, who greeted her with "I believe you have adopted a child." Mary said they had, and invited the visitor in to see the baby. When she had admired the child she told Mary there was something she would like to say to her; that was, to be sure and tell the child, as soon as she was able to understand, that she had been adopted. Mary said that was their intention and asked her why she had called to tell her this. "Well," she said, "I was told the night before I was married, and I would hate anyone else to suffer the shock I suffered."

Both adoptions were legalised and a shortened version of birth certificates issued for the children. Mark thinks this is acceptable for all situations where a birth certificate is necessary. His young son, now almost thirteen years, talks of wanting to be a priest. Mark wonders if he would then have a problem — but is prepared to do battle if the situation arises.

Mary and Mark had a special bedtime story for their two small children. When the little girl wanted a story, they would tell how they flew off in an aeroplane to a place full of babies, and looked everywhere for one they would like to have. They looked and looked and were about to leave, when suddenly they saw her, picked her up, cuddled and loved her and brought her home. They varied it from girl to boy on different nights.

Shortly before their ninth wedding anniversary Mary woke up one morning with a pain in her ribs— not a very bad pain, but she went to see the doctor. After a doubtful looking X-Ray, he told Mark he thought Mary had cancer of the marrow. Ten weeks later she died.

During her illness in a Dublin hospital Mark travelled up each weekend to see her, and a young girl who had been helping Mary with the children began to live in. Mary did not realise she was dying. She never saw the children once she was admitted to hospital. The little girl was now three years, and the boy almost two.

Mark was shattered. His boss moved him to a different town in the south-west. The young help of eighteen moved with them and so they embarked on a period of grief and worry. The girl was devoted to the children but incredibly wasteful and Mark was left to cope with her bad housekeeping. Her late nights were a constant worry to him. His mother, who lived alone in Dublin, was constantly coming and going.

He recalls a visit he had from a Parish Priest

soon after his wife's death. At this stage Mark felt
he had lost faith in God and human nature. The
priest's greeting was "Christ, Mark, you've had a
bellyful and it would make you wonder if there's
a God there at all, after what you've been through
and giving a good home to two children!" Mark
was very emphatic about the impression this made
on him. He feels he would have utterly rejected
any pious platitudes. A nun had sent him a message,
through his sister, that had really upset him. It was
"Tell your brother that God has never made a
mistake — yet."

In loneliness Mark realised how empty of real
understanding his own heart had been towards
other people in sorrow. He came to the conclusion
that visitors directly after a bereavement were not
nearly as helpful as later on, when life went back
to normal. He recalls how he used to sit in front of
his tv, not watching it, with a book on his lap,
while he cried and cried and prayed to God that
someone would ring the doorbell. No one did.

Ten days after he resumed work Mark had a
phone call from his boss, saying he was travelling
down to meet him for lunch. He told Mark that
there did not seem to be any record of the second
child's adoption being legalised. Mark assured him
that all formalities had been fully completed with
regard to both children. The boss went on to say
that pending this confirmation from Mark, the
firm had retained the services of senior Counsel to
fight his case in the High Court, if necessary,
should there be any attempt to take the child from

him. "Knowing you," he said, "I assumed you would wish to keep the children."

Mark never contemplated parting with the children. They gave him something to work for and gave him a reason for battling on. The Christmas after his wife's death he was overwhelmed by the generosity his customers showed to his children. He would come home from each journey laden with gifts for them.

A very striking feature of Mark's experiences seems to be the extraordinary kindness of his firm. Not alone did they make every effort to help him by moving his base, but they showed deep personal concern in such a way that Mark was always conscious of their full support and encouragement. When he later needed advice, it was to one of these men he went, in the knowledge that the advice would be sound and given in genuine love and concern. Mark's father died when he was small and he had no brother.

The little girl, now almost four years old, missed her mother and asked about her. The boy was too young to be affected. Mark tried to tell them that Mummy had gone to God.

For a year after Mary's death Mark never went out in the evening. He had converted the main bedroom into a sitting-room cum play-room for the children and himself. He had the tv there. There was a pub opposite the house and Mark was always afraid that if he left the house the children might be upset by noise or incidents in the street.

When eventually Mark did begin to go out in

the evenings, he only stayed long enough to have two pints with a man friend. He went out really to get away from the house where the young help would sit opposite him at the fire on her nights on.

Soon after this Mark went into an office one day to meet a former friend, who had been newly transferred to the town. His friend was out and Mark was interviewed by a girl, who took his name and message. A week after, on his return to this office, his friend introduced him to the staff of the office, including the only girl who worked there. Mark's friend had already told them all of his circumstances, in case there would be any embarrassment caused by someone asking Mark about his wife.

And so Anne comes into the picture.

Anne is now Mark's wife and is only too happy to talk about her romance. She was barely thirty years old and always regretted she had not met him a few weeks earlier, when she would still have been in her twenties. Mark was thirty-eight.

Anne recalls very clearly that first day when Mark walked into the office. He was, she said, very handsome — a lovely-looking fellow. Well dressed, wearing a hat which he so courteously doffed in greeting, and speaking beautifully in his gentlemanly way. She was immediately attracted to this interesting stranger, but when the boss told his staff his friend's story, she was even more attracted.

Mark describes how he noticed this girl, too. Her eyes were so full of kindness, he said. He thought she must be a very nice girl to have such an expression and such warmth in her smile.

Anne was already involved with two men, of one of whom she was very fond; the other cared for her more than she for him. Once Mark appeared these interests faded. The story of Mark's bereavement and his two adopted children was to her an overwhelming reason for liking him. Mark's business took him into this office several times a week, and so the impressions deepened. They arranged to have a meal together. On that first outing Mark himself told Anne of his first marriage and his children. He also told her he would like to see her again, but would prefer that they travelled out of town, in case Anne would be branded as dating a married man with two children by people who did not know the circumstances. Eventually this charge was made to Mark, when he and Anne were engaged.

Mark would claim that he was not conscious of being on the look-out for a wife. He thought his market was limited at his age. Either the girls were in the eighteen — twenty-three age group and would be mainly interested in jazzing and the gay life, or they would be confirmed spinsters of his own age. As the friendship grew, Mark realised that Anne was every bit as kind as her eyes had promised. If she has a fault, he says, it is that her heart is too big and that she has an insatiable appetite for taking on the impossible, inside and outside her own family circle. He thought his situation would put any girl off.

Anne on the contrary felt drawn to this man, in this situation. Firstly she fell for himself — his courtesy and his fine appearance.

And so they progressed. Anne recalls how on her second date Mark talked and talked and she listened to his every word. "Now," she laughs, "I'm always trying to cut you short."

After a six months' engagement, they were married.

Anne attended a pre-marriage course and had a medical check-up. She never worried that after her marriage Mark might make comparisions, even mentally. She loved him for what he was when she first saw him. The prospect of taking on two children did not bother her at all — in fact enhanced the situation. At nineteen, she could remember looking after her cousin's children for a long weekend. She had adored the baby.

Mark's children were lovely, she said. She recalled the first time she saw them. Mark had asked her to the house. When she appeared in the hallway, a door opened slightly and two little heads appeared round it, the little girl's on top and the boy's underneath. Mark had bathed and prepared them for bed. They immediately became friends.

Anne's father, however, was concerned that perhaps she had not given sufficient thought to the children and they discussed this. She assured him that if there were twelve adopted children she would make the same decision.

Once that was out of the way, everyone rejoiced with the couple and prepared for the wedding. Mark took a trip to Dublin to do three things: buy a ring, tell his mother-in-law, and tell his mother of his intended marriage.

Mary's mother was pleased for him, that he was getting another chance of happiness and that the children would be looked after. She gave him her blessing. She was a widow and Mary had been her only child.

Mark had written to a valued older friend in his firm and was encouraged by the answer he got, advising him to think of his remarriage as a compliment to his dead wife, rather than a disloyalty. Mark had not forgotten his wife, still has not. He prays for her every morning and evening of his life. He loved her deeply, but there has been no conflict of loves. He loves Anne too.

Meanwhile the wedding day was drawing near. Mark was in England on a course and his mother was installed with his children. All arrangements for the honeymoon abroad had been handled by Mark. One of the decisions they made in their talks together was that after their marriage they would have one night out together every month. Mark was always aware that Anne would have rather more to cope with than other young brides. He was alert to her needs, even before she herself recognised them.

Anne never considered she was doing anything great in taking on the two children. She would vehemently deny that there was any hardship in this. She took it in her stride.

And so they wed, with the children joining in

the celebrations. Anne's family consisted of Father, Mother, three sisters and two brothers.

The first day of their continental honeymoon dawned cool and cloudy, so they set out to shop for the family, to get this chore out of the way and enjoy the sun when it would shine. Anne had come away, literally, without a penny in her purse. Mark insisted that it was better to leave him the job of organising travellers' cheques, etc., and he was also careful lest their money be stolen. He knew the attire of slacks and shirts afforded little pocket protection. Anyway, Anne found herself wanting to buy this for Mum and this for Dad — and Mark still holding on to the money. The shopping ended in tears, and silence.

Mark was mad with himself for being so stupid and realised he should have given her some money "into her fist". He figured he had made a silly mistake.

Anne recognised the tiff as one of those things she had been warned to expect on a honeymoon, when a complete change of life and considerable loss of independence could lead to emotional upset. She was grateful for the pre-marriage course.

Next day the sun shone and Mark and Anne enjoyed the remainder of their honeymoon.

At no stage so far, or since, has Anne worried about Mark comparing her to his first wife. Once he actually called her Mary, and she drew his attention to the mistake. They talked about it then, but Anne insists she has never felt threatened or insecure. She has absolute confidence in her love for Mark and his love for her.

Six months of their marriage had passed and Anne did not conceive. They laughingly agreed that it was a good thing they already had two children. Soon afterwards Anne became pregnant and in quick succession had three daughters, with little over a year between the first and second, and again the second and third.

They both love all their children, but Anne felt very tired after the birth of her third daughter. She found the clothes washing, baby feeding and lesson supervision for the older two a great strain. She talked it over with Mark and a priest friend. She then decided to go on the pill for two years and told the Lord she would take as many children as he wanted to send her after that. She has not, in fact, had another child, although she gave up the pill after two years.

Outings together now are very limited. The promised monthly night out was continued until the soaring cost of eating out prompted them to give it up. Both like to play golf, separately and together. Anne dislikes tv and they often play games, like Scrabble, with the children. They like to have family outings to beautiful places in the neighbourhood. They love these outings, and so do the children.

Altogether they are a happy, lively bunch. The two older children love their three young sisters. Anne tells about the day she was going to the hospital for the birth of her third child, and the boy was telling his little sisters, sitting beside him on the floor, how Mummy kept her babies in her tummy. "But me and Jenny," he said, "we were adopted. We were picked out from whole lots of babies." The little girls could not even pronounce "adopt", but whatever it meant, there they were all together, waiting for their new baby.

As they talked together, their compatibility was very obvious. They laughed often. Life must bring problems, but when they talk about their adopted children they are confident that they are happy, well-adjusted children. No personality problems have emerged that would indicate worry or insecurity, and they are now fifteen and thirteen years old.

One thing struck me forcibly and that was the omission of any reference to sexuality in their marriage. When I pointed this out, they both admitted that sexual compatibility was one of the very important elements of their marriage, but in their case it was never a problem. It was just one facet of their relationship and while it is so very important, it does not emerge over any other important approach to budgeting, leisure activities, neighbourliness and the children's interests.

There is plenty of love in this partnership. It flashes between them, in glances exchanged, in their smiles, and maybe most of all — in their sorrow. Mark has suffered deeply. Anne loves him enough to be there always when he needs her, be it in love or in sadness.

5 Paddy and Eileen

Twenty-three years married and now aged forty-five and forty-four respectively, Paddy and Eileen are a settled looking, warmhearted couple. Their experiences of life and marriage have been sometimes harsh, indeed harsh enough to seem unreal. But there is nothing unreal about their love for one another. It shines.

Both Paddy and Eileen are Dublin born and come from large families, of eight and seven children.

Paddy left school after Primary Cert. at the age of fourteen. His father, who was an alcoholic, owned the builders' providers business which had been his father's before him. The drinking habits of the father deprived his family of security, money, food and adequate clothing. Paddy's oldest brother took charge of the business at the age of seventeen. There were frequent rows. Discipline in the home was mostly exercised by the mother, but usually concerned observance of religious duties, like attending Mass on Sundays, going to confession and regular sodalities. Apart from this, Paddy never felt that anyone had much interest in him. He never saw any demonstration of affection between his parents. He pitied his mother. She did not confide in her children.

Paddy went about with a gang of boys, was their ringleader. He chatted up the girls and made contacts for himself and his pals.

One night after a sodality, Paddy and his friends met up with some girls selling flags for a St John Bosco Boys' Club. Paddy took a fancy to the girl with the box and bought the remainder of the flags, on condition she would meet him again. And so she did.

The girl was Eileen.

Another of the gang fancied her too, and Paddy was aware then, and afterwards, that Eileen attracted the boys. She was good-looking and walked well, with her head in the air.

Eileen was not immediately attracted to Paddy. On their first date a pal came with him. Next date, Paddy did not turn up at all and Eileen thought she had seen the last of him. About a month later a fellow at work asked her if she had ever been out with a Paddy O'Shea. When she said she had, he told her that Paddy had been looking all over for her. After this she got a note from Paddy, with a phone number, asking her to ring him. She still has this note.

The night he failed to turn up for his date he had gone out with another girl. He found it hard to get away from his pals. They would sit on him or hold him down, so that he could not leave them to go with Eileen.

Paddy freely admits that he liked girls — always liked girls — liked to kiss them good-night and "a hell of a lot more".

When Eileen started to go out with Paddy she was sixteen. She was a daily communicant at a seven o'clock morning Mass, and when Paddy discovered this he began to attend the same Mass just to see her. They met as often as they could. Eileen had to help at home with washing, ironing and cleaning, on Tuesday nights and Saturdays. Apart from this they met every night, beginning with a novena on Monday nights.

They walked and cycled. On Sundays they would ride far out into the country and take a lunch with them. Sometimes, when funds allowed, they would queue up for the Sunday night pictures. Paddy earned 75p a week as a clerk.

The courtship, however, was not all serene. Paddy soon discovered that while other girls liked to be kissed and fondled, Eileen did not. She steadfastly resisted all advances. He had his face slapped. He was allowed to go home sulking. But he came back every time. Paddy says it was his first experience of resistance and he was determined to break it down. They fought a lot.

Eileen would deny that Paddy was in any way tough. She says he was gentle, really — easy to talk to, and he took a lot of abuse.

For Paddy, it seemed, the more resistance he met the more intense became his desire. After

three years' courtship he still had to fight for his
goodnight kiss. Eileen would not easily allow him
near her, would insist on being kissed while she
stood with her arms folded.

Eileen says Paddy did not make her nervous in
any way. It just seemed as if she was incapable of
relaxing. She was terrified of the unknown, and sex
and love were to her unknown and mysterious
territory. It was about this time that Paddy discovered, one night, that Eileen was totally ignorant
about sex. She thought a passionate kiss would
make her pregnant.

Paddy was incredulous. He grabbed her and
brought her up a lane. Eileen thought something
dreadful was going to happen. He explained that he
needed a dark place, where he could not see her
face, nor she his, so that he could tell her a thing or
two without the two of them suffering acute
embarrassment.

Afterwards Eileen could never remember pre-
cisely what Paddy had said, but she came out of
that alleyway a happier girl. There was still no
question of carte blanche for Paddy, and as he said
himself, until the day they were married he was
being kept severely in his box.

Visiting Eileen's home was a great joy for Paddy.
It was a rowdy, happy household, with father
always there, and always sober. Friends of the
children came and went with absolute freedom.
Often when he and Eileen would be standing at the
front door, in the hallway, or maybe on the stairs,
Eileen's father would call them in for the Rosary.

Everyone in the house at this time had to say the Rosary, the Litany and the Legion prayers. As Paddy said, it was a great incentive for him to leave early and go home.

Meeting Eileen's family accentuated for Paddy his own unhappy home, but Eileen remembers Paddy's father with great affection. He was, she said, the most loving person she ever met. He was kind and gentle. Yes, he had the shakes, could not even hold a cup, took the whisky bottle to bed with him, seemed to drink all night and headed for the pub as soon as he woke in the morning. But as far as the business was concerned he was a great calculator, and could work out timber costs quickly and well.

Eileen here remembers a profoundly moving encounter. Paddy's father had fallen into the fire and his arm was severely burned. It became gangrenous and had to be amputated. While he was in hospital Eileen went to visit him. His wife was there. When visiting time was up the wife moved away from the bed. The sick man caught Eileen's arm and asked her if she would do him a favour. Would she tell that woman gone out the door that he loved her very, very deeply? Tears were running down his face. Eileen caught up with the woman, who asked her what the man had wanted. Eileen gave her message. The woman said "Ach, a lot of rubbish." Eileen was terribly upset by this encounter, by the hopelessness of the situation. The woman had suffered so much that it was now too late to change things. Eileen had sympathy for the woman and understood her hardness. She did not blame her.

When the man came out of hospital, Eileen visited their home very often. By this time he was doubly incapacitated by the loss of the arm and increasingly severe shakes. Eileen and her children would take him out for walks in the park. He died not long afterwards.

So much for Paddy and his unhappy father. As for his mother, who is still alive, he is not close to her in the same way as his own children are to himself and Eileen. He is sorry for his mother, but it does not seem as if this woman easily accepts sympathy or love. She has had a sad and bitter experience from which she has emerged, perhaps, but will never recover fully.

For Paddy there seemed to be everything in Eileen's home in terms of affection, friendliness and hospitality.

Their courtship lasted for five years and was marked by rows, separations and problems about keeping their relationship under control, when there was no immediate prospect of getting married.

Paddy could never save. Eileen was good at managing. Paddy eventually handed Eileen his savings each week. She would keep it in the house, but soon discovered that this would not work. Her mother would borrow a bit to help dress some child for first communion or something similar. She would mean to pay it back, but never did. Eileen would try to make good the loss herself.

Paddy would get frustrated by the ups and downs
of restraint and saving. Several times he gave up
and went with other girls. Once they broke up for
two months; another time for four months. Eileen
felt desperately lonely when they parted. She knew
she loved Paddy. She would ask our Lady to send
him back.

Paddy gave Eileen a ring, mostly to warn off any
other fellow who might put his eye on her, and in
a way to restrict her and mark her out as "his".
Sometimes he would get involved with his pals and
miss dates. More rows. Eileen gave him back the
ring and for six miserable weeks they parted again.

Paddy had no one to turn to in his problems. His
family did not know he planned to marry. He
would go to confession and tell the priest about
this girl he hoped to marry, but could not get
enough money together. He would admit that he
found it hard to control his emotions. The priest
told him he must give up this girl who was an
occasion of sin — and not to come back until he
had. Eileen would never allow Paddy to do more
than kiss her goodnight. Paddy, for all his way-
wardness with girls, had never had intercourse.
Until he was married he did not fully appreciate
the risks he had taken.

Babies were never discussed in their talks before
marriage. Family planning was only mentioned
when Eileen had her second child and a miscarriage.
Only then did they wonder how many children
they wanted.

Their wedding was celebrated at Eileen's home.

The honeymoon was disastrous. They went away after the wedding and Eileen was still almost totally ignorant. Her mother had never discussed sex with her. She had completely misunderstood the necessity of choosing a suitable wedding date, so that she went off on her honeymoon with her mother's ambiguous comment still in her ears: "You'll have to tell Paddy to wait another few days." She was either sick or crying for three days — and they came back.

When they did have their first intercourse it was a wonderful experience for both. They were relaxed and leisurely. For the inhibited Eileen it was a revelation, for Paddy the culmination of years of frustration, disappointment, even hopelessness. Both considered it was well worth the wait and the trials to achieve such perfect enjoyment.

Not for long were their days untroubled. There was no house available and both were determined to get somewhere they could be alone together. They ended up with two rooms in a house owned by spinster sisters, on the understanding that they move as soon as possible.

One baby and a year afterwards they were still in two rooms, being harassed by the sisters. Their light and their water supply were cut off. Paddy asked the sisters to be patient and not to torment his wife. Eileen took to wheeling the baby to her own house in the morning and returning to the rooms with Paddy in the evening. Sometimes they were locked out. The baby got pneumonia and was six months in hospital.

Relief seemed in sight when some man Paddy knew went to England and left his Corporation house. Paddy borrowed £55 in the bank and bought the key. In two weeks the Corporation turned them out. Sale of a key was illegal, and other couples with more children were higher on the waiting list.

They spent two weeks apart then, he with his family, she with hers. Then their name came up in a Corporation draw and they were given a maisonette. It was like heaven to be on their own with their baby, and expecting another one. And so they spent four happy years.

It was about then that Eileen noticed a vacant house, and Paddy wrote his application to the Corporation. Another £50 was needed for the down payment, and the former £55 was still being repaid to the bank. Paddy's family could have helped but thought that people in Paddy's position should be content to rent a house, not to buy one. They refused. Eileen's father lent them the £50, so they moved into the house where they still live. This was eighteen years ago. It is now a happy home for themselves and their six children.

In the first years of their marriage Eileen had one very serious problem of her own, apart from money and housing. When she already had three children and was six years married, she was one day travelling on a bus. She held her baby in her arms, and on either side of her sat her two older children. Two women sat on the opposite seat. One was saying "Hasn't she got the beautiful children?"

"Yes," answered the other, "they're gorgeous kids. And that baby's a beauty."

"It's the likes of her would have them," said the first woman. "What do you mean?" asked the other.

"Do you not know who your woman is? Well, you know the ones used to live up the road there," and proceeded to tell the family history for everyone on the bus to hear. Eileen was in a terrible state. She couldn't help thinking what a shock the conversation would have been to Paddy, if he'd been with her. She had never told him the family history.

She got off the bus before her stop and walked to meet Paddy who was waiting to help her with the children. He could see she was very upset, and asked her what had happened. She could not tell him there and then, and with his usual sensitive, trusting love, he urged her to set her mind at rest and tell him what was troubling her whenever and if ever she felt like it. One night, about a month after this, they were in bed and had made love. Lying there afterwards, Eileen told Paddy she would like to talk.

Her mother was fourteen years old and already pregnant when she married her father, who was sixteen. They ran away to get married and returned penniless and homeless. Her mother had been received into the Catholic Church after her marriage and now had to bring her new husband back to her own home, where they got accommodation and disapproval. There the young couple stayed until Eileen's mother was twenty-one, when she inherited a lot of money from her grandmother and they moved out to their own home. They had seven children.

When Eileen was eight her father joined the army, and soon afterwards her mother went out one day and did not come back. There was a baby of a few weeks in the house. Grannies, aunts and cousins took the children. When her father came home for a night and saw the situation he was furious. Mother was brought home and there was a terrible row.

Soon after this she was sent to prison for deserting her children. And so the pattern continued. Mother came and went. Children were farmed out. The last time Eileen's mother disappeared, Eileen and her brother decided to keep the children together. There was no small baby this time. The younger children never knew where their mother was. She was often ill, so hospital was an acceptable explanation.

Eileen remembers when her grandmother would insist on taking her out with her to look for her mother. She hated having to go. She was twelve years old when, one day, her search ended in a tenement room of unspeakable squalor, where four women lay in one bed and a man and a woman in another. Her granny would stay outside and send Eileen in. The women in the room told Eileen's mother to get rid of that kid as fast as she could, and so Eileen was told to get out and not to come back. Her mother told her not to tell granny that she had found her, and that she was not coming back.

Eileen ran out of the place, back to her granny, trying to hide her tears and pretend she had not seen her mother. Eileen says her father never knew she was being sent on messages of this kind. She was always ashamed to speak of her mother and never had the courage to speak of her to a living soul.

Finally, when Eileen was fourteen years old, her mother came home and stayed. And so, when Paddy came on the scene, he saw only the happy family who contrasted so vividly with his own.

When Paddy heard Eileen's story he felt no resentment, only a profound compassion for her sufferings. He had known there was some skeleton in the cupboard, but nothing of its nature. As he said, he was mad about Eileen and married *her*, not her father and mother. But now he understood many things about Eileen, her fears and stand-offishness.

Eileen remembers the night she told Paddy everything about herself and her family. She felt she was only then a real married person. There would be no more holding back, no fear of exposure such as she had suffered on the bus. There was nothing left unspoken between them and no matter what the future held, they would meet it together. They had their own home, their own children and their very precious love.

Now that Eileen had given herself completely to

Paddy they embarked on a strangely new marriage, full of joy and thanksgiving.

Paddy in his turn did not condemn Eileen's mother. He felt she had married very young, had a houseful of children and no privacy. He thought she had been desperately deprived and just couldn't take it.

At this stage he told Eileen some of his own childhood hardships when bills were owing everywhere. He, too, had been sent to a tenement to pay a bill. He was ten years old and had been appalled at the utter filth and desolation of these houses. He suffered anew for Eileen when he discovered that she had been exposed to such unutterable miseries.

Paddy recalled again how he had loved the atmosphere in Eileen's house. They laughed about the grab for broken biscuits at tea-time on a Sunday afternoon, and the way all boy and girl friends had to be brought home for inspection.

Now they marvelled that so much suffering could so wonderfully heal and seem never to have happened.

Eileen's father was often concerned that his children would not blame him for what happened. Eileen would emphasise that she was not interested in apportioning blame. She only knew that her parents' differences had left her friendless and open to vicious, cutting jibes. She was always on the defensive. Even when she was in hospital after a miscarriage, the woman in the next bed told her one day that she would never understand how Eileen had not turned out "bad". She complained that she had six children and out of those six, she was quite sure four could be termed delinquent. "My children," she said, "came from a good home and look at you and the children you had."

But to get back to Paddy and Eileen. In the twenty-three years of their marriage Eileen had thirteen pregnancies. Her menstrual cycle was so abnormal that the rhythm method of birth control was never fully successful. During her pregnancies, and on account of her disposal to miscarry, Paddy was often without intercourse for nine months at a stretch. Consequently there were many strains and stresses.

Coitus interruptus was a recurring problem. Eileen had very strong views about restraint. She felt that if she could not have intercourse they should not make love. And yet she believed it was her duty never to refuse Paddy, and also not to be a source of temptation. In confession she would try and explain her problems. Once she was told it was her fault and that she was an occasion of sin to her husband, and this after fourteen years of marriage.

Both Paddy and Eileen were enthusiastic about a retreat for married couples that they attended. It was a one-day retreat. Paddy was talking to the priest about their problem. They left that retreat much relieved. The priest explained that as long as their intentions were genuinely unselfish and that they both desired to make one another happy and not just satisfy their selfishness, they should be loving towards one another. Since then, Paddy and

Eileen prefer to talk over their problems with a priest who knows them, rather than take their chance in the confessional. They do not feel a personal encounter with a priest means a free pardon, but that their genuine contrition for any lapse will be judged in the light of their circumstances and good intentions.

Their youngest child is now ten years and in the past few months they have been using the calendar method of birth control, and feel more confident of its accuracy. On medical grounds Eileen would never contemplate the pill.

It was not until they became involved in talks with pre-marriage couples that Eileen and Paddy learned of the temperature method. They feel that they have learned a lot in the last ten years. Added to her difficult menstrual cycle, her dangerous and debilitating miscarriages, Eileen suffers from migraine.

Paddy suffers with her. He hates to see her pregnant or sick — which has often been the same thing. She pretends she has not her headache, but he always knows by her face that she is in pain and refrains from causing her any further discomfort.

Another serious problem they encountered was Eileen's continual resistance to uninhibited love making. Paddy was often enraged by her mundane comments about light bills and gas bills, when he was already transported to another world. He was also very upset by her consistent failure to take the initiative in their love making. Even when they were already fifteen years married he was often uncertain whether or not she really loved him, because she was continually putting up barriers between them. And so he decided he would completely reverse his behaviour. He would go to bed and settled down to sleep without a goodnight kiss. She knew she had done nothing to annoy him. She would ask him what was the matter. She got no satisfactory answer. He would be pleasant and kind in the daytime but would freeze up at night and seem reluctant even to talk.

Eventually she put her arms about him one night and asked him to talk to her. Paddy pointed out that it was the first time, in fifteen years of marriage, that she had made any advance towards him. Eileen tried to explain that she loved him very much but that she could not bring herself to make the advances. She promised to try very hard to improve. Paddy promised to be patient and helpful, so that she might overcome the very real difficulty she had.

Both know now that there is no question about their love, only that Eileen finds it hard to express her love in the same way he does. Probably she will always have this difficulty, but with goodwill on both sides they feel this problem should eventually disappear.

Sexual expression is a very important feature of this marriage. An ability to talk things out, anything and everything, to object, disagree or disapprove, is very important. There is a great sense of humour between them.

Prayer matters very much to both. Paddy was

always in the habit of praying by his bedside. He always seemed to be asking forgiveness for something. He often thought he was, essentially, a bad person. The Rosary had been a feature of his own up-bringing. Even when he was quite ill Paddy's father would have the Rosary beads in his bed and in his hands when he woke up in the morning.

Eileen prayed a lot, but said her night prayers in bed. Paddy came to realise that when she was quiet and not talking, she was praying. Now they often hold hands and pray together.

About their children Paddy regrets that they do not have the family Rosary. He feels it is basic to family life.

Eileen points out that in her own home they were made to say the Rosary, and often grudged the obligation of reporting in time for it. They would not dare miss it, their father was so rigid about it. Eileen likes to talk to her children about God, and prayer, and being Christian. She thinks it's important to take young children up in your arms, or on your knees, and talk to them about God.

Some time ago Eileen found herself with a prayer-group of children, her own and others from the road. She began by reading pieces from a prayer book for her own children, who asked if they could bring their pals. Ages ranged from eight to eighteen and soon the group numbered between forty and fifty. Eileen had to stop from lack of space, but even more because she felt she was not capable of coping with the children's questions.

Paddy and Eileen feel that their children have passed them out educationally and know more than they do about the Bible, and they regret this.

Paddy's work pattern has changed over the years. He now offers his clerical services independently of any one firm and finds this affords him freedom, a better way of life and considerable job satisfaction.

Both Paddy and Eileen feel that it is important that they should go out together. They are very much involved in the Christian Family Movement and Marriage Encounter. They supply other young couples with baby sitters from their own family and say this is a feature of the sharing involved in being interested in these groups. Eileen and Paddy have never gone out separately and were always able to get sisters and relations to baby sit for them when the children were young.

They feel that young women should make a special effort to go out with their husbands regularly and think that it is often the start of serious trouble when the young wife is too busy or too content at home to accompany her young husband who wants to go out.

It seems that the people who meet for these marriage groups are prepared to talk frankly to each other about all the aspects of their family life. The discuss things like money, children or sex. There is no pettiness and no talking outside about one another's problems. There is always a priest with the group and Paddy and Eileen feel that they, in their own way, have much to contribute. Having the ability to talk freely about themselves, they find it encourages others who have problems to take them out into the open and talk.

Eileen thinks money is a very important feature in marriage. Their first real row was about money. Paddy, for a period of several years, had become a gambler. Looking back he thinks he must have been crazy. His gambling caused Eileen great hardship in terms of money and unpaid bills. He himself was completely hooked on horses. It began with an unexpectedly substantial win and then he spent months trying to repeat the victory. He was late for meals, he could not read the newspaper past the racing pages. He would come home with jam, cheese, and biscuits and tins of pears when he would have a win. Eileen never thanked him for these luxuries because, naturally enough, she would have preferred the money to pay the bills.

Once he came home very excited about a dead cert for a race the next day. He implored Eileen to give him the money she was gathering to pay a bill. But Eileen refused. The horse won and Paddy was furious. Soon after he came along with a similar request and reminded Eileen that if she had listened to him the first time, she would not only have enough for the bill, but could buy things they needed as well. Anyway, she relented. The horse lost.

Eileen's main concern during this period was their marriage and their happiness. They were drifting towards disaster. Paddy was a different man. As he says himself, he might as well have been an alcoholic. His mother and brothers were always interested in

horses and betting and at one stage Eileen went to
them and asked them to refrain from giving Paddy
tips, or even discussing races at all. Paddy was
deeply hurt that she would go to his family in this
way.

At this time Paddy felt keenly that he was not
levelling in the marriage group situation. He felt he
was hardly Christian and even if gambling was
mentioned, he could switch off and tell himself it
did not concern him. He even felt he was justified in
compensating himself in this way for the restrictions
the rhythm method of birth control imposed on
him.

He never sent any of his children into a bookie's
to place a bet and thought he was fooling them all
along with his various excuses for being late in or
missing meals. One day they were all in a bus and
one of the children pointed to a bookie's office and
asked loudly "Is that where my Daddy works?" As
Paddy laughingly put it, that was a queer kick in the
pants. Paddy was now earning more than he had
ever dreamed possible and here he was frittering it
away.

By the grace of God, this problem is now safely
tucked away in the memories of Paddy and Eileen as
a bad experience, but one from which they finally
emerged together.

This couple have thirty years' relationship behind
them. There have been love, problems and tragedies.
Perhaps there are more difficulties ahead. But I
doubt if anything could now shake their love
for one another. Eileen's love has a quality of dev-

otion, but at the same time she is an outspoken woman who will always disagree if she has to.

Paddy sometimes sounds tough, maybe aggressive. But he is as vulnerable as Eileen. Their love exposes them to hurt and disappointment, but it is also their glory.

It seemed to me like some beautiful flower thriving in grimy soil.

6 Maeve and Peter

We were in a long, elegant sitting room, with pale walls, big windows and deep comfortable chairs. One armchair was pushed crookedly into a far corner, and Peter explained that he had broken it.

Looking at this broad, long-legged young man, I thought it would take a good chair to hold him. We were laughing as we settled down to talk.

On ski slopes in Scotland Maeve and Peter met for the first time.

Maeve, then twenty-six, was doing a line with the ski-instructor.

Peter, aged twenty-seven, was invited along by the ski-instructor's brother, who was his friend.

When Maeve first met Peter in a pub after a day's skiing, she was immediately aware of this stranger with the twinkling brown eyes and made a mental note of inviting him to a party she was having the following week. She was thinking how he would be a "real catch" for one of her girl friends.

Three months later Peter heard that Maeve was

having another party in her parents' home, and decided to invite himself along, feeling fairly sure that Maeve would be glad to see him. In the intervening three months, Peter had done a line with another girl.

At the party Maeve and Peter paired up and five months later were unofficially engaged. And so began the difficulties inherent in a mixed marriage situation. Maeve was the only daughter of a Presbyterian minister. She had one brother.

Peter was a Catholic whose parents were both alive, as were his brother and sister.

Peter's father was a liberal-minded man and did not worrry unduly about the prospect of Peter's marriage. Mother, however, was different. Steeped as she was in strong Catholic traditions, she thought her son's marriage to a Presbyterian would be a disaster.

Maeve's father and mother never put any difficulties in her way, because they were both strongly attracted to Peter as a person. The first time she had brought Peter home, Maeve's mother said "Do you know that's the nicest young man you've ever brought to this house — and he has to be a Catholic." Maeve's father was not by nature a bigot. He pointed out to them the difficulties they would have to encounter, such as the pre-marriage promise about the children. He gave them his blessing. Again, Peter's own charm and personality were important factors.

Peter and Maeve were aware, however, of the embarrassment a Presbyterian minister would suffer, not alone at the marriage ceremony, but pastorally and socially in many other ways.

Maeve's mother had grave misgivings about the mixed marriage situation. Having the experience of the two unfortunate mixed marriages in her own family and thinking in terms of pre-Vatican regulations, she thought Irish Catholic families were completely dominated by their priests. She thought too that it was utterly degrading for couples to be married "in porches" and being forced to "sign things" — all because other Churches were considered inferior to the Catholic Church. She saw possible unhappiness for Maeve in trying to cope with interference from priests concerning her children.

Peter laughingly says that Maeve copes very well with the priests and has found that, in fact, priests do not interfere.

It seemed as if this courtship and marriage were entirely overshadowed by their differing religious beliefs. Once an engagement was even contemplated, the couple was under strain. Relations took over, bringing out objections, revealing sometimes real nastiness, which at times spilled over the unfortunate pair and was, to say the least, a constant irritation.

As Peter and Maeve said, it was no wonder people in similar circumstances turned against parents and Churches and finally emerged irretrievably lost to one, or other, or both.

Such a situation in courtship deprived them of a leisurely period in which to get to know one another, and made them ever conscious of the hurt and annoyance they were causing to their families.

A typical example of the tensions involved was the couple's first visit together to a priest to discuss their marriage. As Peter said, he was very conscious as a Catholic of the reactions his partner might have to whatever the priest would say. They were both extremely tense. The priest, in his turn, did not appreciate these tensions and Peter feels that in this area the priests themselves are uneasy, and therefore less able to handle the difficulties.

A priest in such a situation, continued Peter, has to tell the non-Catholic partner what are the rules of the Catholic Church, and has to try to suggest that the children should be brought up Catholics. Such a job is not easy for the priest, but it is possible to handle it diplomatically — depending on the priest. There are dispensations necessary. There is a form to be filled. You get the impression that an immense favour is being bestowed on you. Also if the couple desires any difference in the marriage ceremony, such as not wishing to have Nuptial Mass, another dispensation from canonical form is required. This means more forms and consequently more delay.

Maeve admits to being scared of meeting the Parish Priest for the first time. She says they were not a typical mixed marriage couple, insofar as her father was a minister. The priest was cool — but very nice, really.

Maeve also felt resentful that so many barriers

were raised by Peter's Church. After all, what was wrong with *her*? Much strain in this way was put on Peter, who had to try to smooth out these problems for Maeve.

But both Peter and Maeve agree that there are extremely good things about this "mixed" experience. Each partner's religion is on trial to the other and so tends to make each look more closely at his beliefs. Peter says, for instance, he had to try and explain why his Church had seven sacraments.

Also, it helps partners to become more ecumenically minded. You learn at first hand about the other's Church. When Peter went with Maeve to a Presbyterian service, he saw old myths exploded. And similarly, when Maeve went to Mass with Peter. As Maeve said, she was firstly impressed more by the similarities of the Churches than the differences.

The words of both communion services were the same. Peter found the Presbyterian communion service extremely moving and very solemn. He thinks this is because Presbyterian communion is less frequent. There is the table, with the minister behind, and six elders on either side, typifying the twelve apostles. Ordinary bread is broken and eaten, and wine distributed in many chalices, making the symbolism of the Last Supper complete. Symbolism seems to Peter to be important to the Presbyterians.

This is not to say, however, that in ordinary circumstances Peter would adopt Presbyterian traditions. He loves Maeve who is a Presbyterian, and so wants to find out at first hand all that he can about Presbyterians. For him this is a very positive thing.

For Maeve — she accepts that part of the Peter she loves is his Catholic faith. She would not wish him to change, nor does he wish that she should change. Neither could contemplate change just for the sake of making things easier. This would be completely out of character for both Maeve and Peter, who are each practising members of their differing religions.

Peter regards his faith as precious and central to his Irish culture. He says he is less concerned with the idea of the one, true Church than with his Church as part of his cultural heritage. In the light of his marriage experience, Peter says he is more inclined to the idea of a Church catholic, rather than a Catholic Church. He feels he has a better understanding of the Christian Church now that he knows more about other Churches. Also he thinks that his beliefs are stronger because of being forced to examine a different faith.

Neither Maeve nor Peter would condemn anyone for their beliefs. Neither has felt strong criticism among their respective friends, but they feel this sort of atmosphere is less likely in an urban setting anyway.

Maeve laughs as she remembers some friends who said that "Even if her bloke was a smashing fellow, after all — an Irish Catholic! One must draw the line somewhere." No rancour here.

Maeve and Peter admit to having been, at one

time, over sensitive about people's reactions. They feel this is not so bothersome now.

Before they were married Peter and Maeve decided they would like to have four children and that they did not want to start a family immediatly after their marriage. Neither did they attach much importance to things like a fridge, or a dining room suite. They prefered to enjoy their first year of marriage together, and worry about everything else afterwards. Peter always found it irritating listening to parents and others reminiscing about their "struggles". He maintained that one does not necessarily have to struggle, it was more, perhaps, a question of priorities.

Peter had some experiences of sex before marriage and had not found it satisfactory. He was secretly anxious lest he and Maeve should have problems. Therefore, they agreed to have sex before marriage and this proved entirely successful, not only in allaying Peter's fears, but in achieving a closeness that was tremendous in their often troubled pre-marriage days.

While their own experience proved right for them, Maeve and Peter would not generalise about sex before marriage. They feel it all depends on the couple and that sex is a very individual thing. Maeve was very keen to stabilise their sex relationship before marriage, but not until their engagement was firmly established. She felt it took pressure off a potentially problematical area and was doubly important for them, faced as they were with a difficult marriage service.

Also, Maeve was on the pill, because in this matter too she wanted to be fully organised.

Both Maeve and Peter think sex is a very important part of marriage. A honeymoon was also important. At first they decided to take a few days off and go back to work. Both are graduates. But eventually they decided on a decent holiday abroad and think it was a really wonderful, romantic experience. All problems were overcome. They relaxed and enjoyed themselves.

Maeve laughs about a honeymoon tiff, on the last day of their honeymoon in fact. They had gone on a bus ride and Peter was annoyed because some fellow had insisted on talking to Maeve all the time. Peter thought the man was trying to pick her up, while Maeve felt she was being polite in not ignoring the stranger. They sorted it out anyway, and did not allow a one-hour episode to destroy an otherwise perfect honeymoon.

Back to Scotland then and both resumed work. Maeve soon found her situation needed adjustment. She now calls it her "door-slamming" phase. Now that she had her small house to keep and husband to feed, as well as having her job, she found she was never done. They would both come home together in the evening and she would prepare the meal. Then when they were sitting down for a while, Peter would rouse himself and say "Ah — to bed." Maeve found herself with the dirty supper dishes, the milk bottles to leave out and the breakfast table to set for the morning — and she, too, feeling tired. So she took to slamming the doors in frustration. Soon Peter got the message and realised he had done "something" wrong. It had simply never occurred to him to help. They can laugh about it now.

Another problem was Peter's weekend rugby playing. On Saturday mornings they could lie in and rest. Peter would bring up toast and tea to Maeve in bed — and then take off for his game. She had to clean the house, arrange the washing for the launderette, and do the many chores she did not get time to do during the week. Eventually she cut down her work to four days a week. This left her Monday at home and plenty of time to do a general clean-up and also gave her freedom to go out with Peter at the weekend.

While they had little rows, they never have had a serious falling out. Peter gave up the rugby after two years.

It always seems as if Peter was looking out for things that might upset Maeve, and trying to avoid them. When the time came for her to have her first baby, he sought around for a suitable hospital, where she would not meet up with nuns. She had never any previous contact with nuns and Peter felt it was better that she should meet them at another time, when she was more able to cope.

As they had always anticipated, the baptism of their first child was a most traumatic experience for both Maeve and Peter. They were trying to make a decision as to whether the child should be brought up Catholic or Presbyterian. The pre-marriage promise about the children did not solve their problem, rather it complicated it.

The promise, as far as both were concerned, was of intent. If the promise had required a positive undertaking about the baptism, it would have imposed a dreadful strain and would have had some definite effect on their plans. One thing they were agreed on, though; it would never have separated them or prevented the marriage. But the promise suggested that Peter would do all in his power to have the children brought up in the Catholic faith, which he did not consider constituted a firm promise to do any one specific thing. At the time of the promise there was a degree of tension involved, but once it was signed and out of the way the tension eased.

Now, however, there remained the dilemma of the baptism. Time passed, and eventually it was Maeve who one day took herself to visit the local priest. She asked him to show her the order of the service of baptism, so that she could find out if there was anything in it offensive to her Presbyterian beliefs. The priest took out some papers and looking down along them, mumbled here and there, "Well, that doesn't concern you. And this doesn't concern you." Maeve was infuriated that the priest failed to realise the importance for her of her first child's baptism, and pointed out that there was simply no question that any part of the child's baptism did not concern her. She thought, again, that she was being made to feel inferior.

Both parents were anxious that their child

should be baptised openly in their parish church. Friends had coped with a similar situation by having their children baptised by order priests in the oratories of their religious houses.

The baptism eventually took place in the parish Catholic church. No parents or guests were invited. Peter wished to guard against any word or expression that would indicate satisfaction on the Catholic side, and offend Maeve.

The second child's baptism, however, was a much happier occasion. In the intervening space of about three years, Maeve and Peter had learned a lot. They were more sure of themselves and made a careful study as to how to achieve their objective. Eventually they were permitted to have an ecumenical service, attended by Maeve's father and the local priest.

Much thought is being given to the question of the children's religious up-bringing. It seemed important that the children would be prepared for the influence of two Christian denominations and that their baptism should reflect this duality. This is the practicality of the matter.

Now that the baptism has been achieved, there comes the problem of school. Maeve and Peter feel quite sure of their own situation, but fear that there might be some confusion for a child in a two-Church household. They feel, however, that when the child has a warm, strong home atmosphere, he should be able to override anything he encounters in school.

Again, Peter and Maeve want their children

brought up according to the beliefs of one central denomination, being exposed to the other second denomination by going to Mass or church on Sundays — depending on which religion was eventually decided upon.

Peter would not mind the children being brought up Presbyterians, but would like to see them with *one* firm religious programme and members of one established Church. He feels there would be a danger of the children opting out of religion altogether if they were allowed to drift between two Churches.

Prayer, Peter admits, is a difficult area. He has been accustomed to saying set Catholic prayers like the Rosary. Maeve likes to read the Bible and pray "off the cuff". Peter could never see himself reading the Bible, nor Maeve saying the Rosary, so there is a vacuum here. In the beginning they used to say the Our Father together, but do not say it now. Peter is dissatisfied with their present prayer life, and feels it is a problem yet to be solved. They say Grace before and after meals, and morning and night prayers with their three-year-old son.

They feel that God is very important to them both, and that if some real problem arose they might pray together about it. Now that they have two small children, Peter and Maeve go to Church in turns. While Maeve never misses out when it is her turn, Peter admits that Maeve has to dig him out occasionally, to go to Sunday Mass.

Even before they were formally engaged there was one all-important aspect of their future, and that was the matter of inter-Church communion. It

had always seemed unacceptable to Maeve that she
was not welcomed to communion and that she
would not be able to communicate with her own
children in Peter's Church.

The inter-communion problem is still very real
and fundamental — is really one of their big
stumbling-blocks. Maybe, they say, some solution
will evolve with time. Perhaps Maeve will grow
stronger and more secure as the years go by, and
will not continue to be shattered by her inability
to receive communion with her children. Many of
their problems have seemed to lessen with time and
experience. Maeve hopes that somewhere along the
line there will be new developments regarding the
eucharist. It is really a very great sadness to her as
things stand.

Peter and Maeve do not entirely agree as to
whether or not a woman should have other interests
outside the home. Peter complains that Maeve
refused a week in Paris with him, because she
would not leave her one-year-old son. He would
like to see her taking up some other interest, so
that she would be less in danger of becoming
entirely immersed in babies and housewifery. He
fears that her intellect might deteriorate without
the challenge of using her mind.

Maeve feels her first child will soon be going to
school and away from her. She would feel cheated
to miss any of his growing-up, feels she would really
be the loser. She might consider voluntary work
for a few evenings in the week, so that her life
would be less self-centred.

Anyway, the household chores already take her all her time. She wonders how she would cope with a job outside her home. Maeve has strong views about so-called "liberation". She cannot accept her own "liberation" at the cost of some other woman, who would have to come in to relieve her. In this she sees a flaw in the argument for women working outside the home. Some women may need this outlet and become easier to live with when they can escape their household chores, but she feels no need for this sort of escape.

Maeve and Peter go out together as often as once a week, sometimes more. They celebrate birthdays, anniversaries, go to dress dances, dinner dances, plays, an opera or concert. They visit friends in their own homes for meals and they in turn entertain friends in theirs. Baby-sitting is no problem — neighbours and girls living near are always available. Maeve has started to play squash since her second baby was born.

With five years of marriage behind them and two young sons to bring up, Maeve and Peter have everything they set out to have. Their children have been spaced, there have been no problems about birth-control. Their mixed-marriage situation has forced them to plan ahead and foresee problems. They have suffered, but they have also gained considerable experience. They like to help others in their own position and seem to gather great strength from people like themselves. It seems that this sharing of common problems has been a definite help. Peter thinks it has substituted the pastoral care that priests and ministers do not seem able to provide — not from lack of interest as much as genuine inability to relate to the mixed marriage.

When Peter thinks that Maeve might be too immersed in her home and children, he loves to come home and hear about the day's adventures and misadventures. He would laughingly add that he's often quite glad to get back to work on Monday morning after the trials of the weekend.

As with all the other couples I have met a sense of humour is very evident, and recognised as an important factor in marriage.

Sex, while important, can be latent for periods when babies are demanding. Here there is not worry. This area of their lives is leisurely.

Maeve and Peter realise that their situation is likely to produce more problems, especially in view of the fact that their two small children have not yet started school.

They have youth and intelligence and they sincerely want God to be in their home, their hearts and their children's lives.

7 Donal loses Nell

It was bedtime for the little six-year-old girl, Monica. She pushed her doll's pram around the kitchen and was pretending not to notice her Daddy talking about the time. Two other children were doing their lessons at the kitchen table, while a washing machine whirred in the background. Monica was trying to open a little umbrella to protect her dolly from the rain. Golden ringlets were squeezing out of the dotted blue kerchief she wore around her lovely head. Her eyes sparkled as her little face reflected the chasing expressions of curiosity and mischief.

Eventually she said good-night and Donal settled down to tell me his story. Nell and he had married when he was twenty-eight years old and she was twenty-four. Both came from rural backgrounds and both had degrees. Nell had just started in her first job when she gave it up to get married. There was never any question about her continuing work after she was married. It just wasn't thought of in those days of 1962.

Money was scarce after Donal and Nell bought their first house in the suburbs of Dublin, and it was a year before they owned their first car. They were fifteen months married when their first child was born.

Both were delighted about the baby. They were an easy going couple and were very happy. Nell was a bit more ambitious than Donal and often referred to the fact that he did not push himself forwards in his job situation. This was never a serious issue and it was more in the nature of affectionate banter than criticism.

Much as Nell loved having her baby son, she immediately started to enquire how she could space her family. Her gynaecologist, a married man who had no family of his own, was a bit disapproving, and pointed out that there were many couples who longed for children but were not able to have them. However, he gave her full information about the rhythm method of birth control, but three months later Nell was pregnant and became depressed and generally down in the dumps.

Suburban life did not suit either Donal or Nell. They had a nice house, with a view, but they never felt themselves part of the locality. They had very few friends outside their own families, who did not live in Dublin. Consequently they always hoped they would be able to move out of Dublin, and so they did. The week their second child was born, Donal was transferred down the country, where they have lived since.

Two and a half years after the house move, their first daughter and third child was born. Life was good and theirs was a very happy, relaxed household. Donal thinks that they were probably happier than average, and were increasingly aware of their growing relationship.

Leisure time was often spent separately. Nell and Donal both played bridge, but they played together only occasionally, one or other staying at home with the children. Being one of nine himself Donal was always good about the house. He would cook and change nappies and he was very proud of the fact that the children confided equally in himself and Nell.

When their little girl was over four years old, Nell was bothered by a pain for which the doctors could find no explanation. She was sent to Dublin for exhaustive tests, but nothing showed up. Around this time they had been planning to have another child. Nell held back, hoping that either the pain would go, or that something would be diagnosed and she could be rid of the trouble. She was sent home from Dublin with a clean bill of health, although she still had a grumbling pain. Their second daughter was born a year after, when Nell was thirty-four.

This little girl was a great joy and an added happiness to an already happy family. Her birth seemed to have restored Nell to full health. It was summertime and the baby was so contented and winsome that picnics and outings were a great pleasure. The basket would be set in the shade of a tree and the others enjoyed the lovely days and played and swam together.

During that happy summer they had a visit from Donal's brother, who was in Ireland on his honeymoon. This newly-wed couple were all over one another as Donal put it, and he and Nell used to laugh at them. One day the brother asked Donal why he and Nell never showed their love for one another. "Wait till you are eleven years married and see if you can be as happy together as we are," said Donal. He felt this put his brother thinking. There was a great easy-going tempo to their lives at this stage.

Then Nell got a severe recurrence of pain. She was sent back to Dublin for further tests and again she was sent home. By this time the doctors showed more than a hint of impatience. Nell knew they were increasingly inclined to consider her pain as psychological, and she found this terribly distressing. Just before Christmas she was again admitted to hospital. Donal was on his own down the country, wondering how to manage the Christmas holidays.

The three older children went to stay with Nell's sister, and Donal set off for Dublin with the baby to stay with his own sister. Neighbours were very kind at this stage and helped out in many ways. On Christmas day, with the small Monica wrapped up in a yellow suit and looking like a new chick, Donal brought her to the hospital when he went to visit Nell. She, miserable as she was in the grip of that awful pain, could hardly

look at the child. The other women in the ward
were in raptures over the beautiful child. Donal
was racked with pity and disappointment. He went
back to his sister's that Christmas Day and cried.

The surgeon decided to operate on Nell on
New Year's Day and before the operation she was
submitted to a psychological assessment. The
session laster twenty minues and the psychiatrist
failed to find any sign of psychological disorder.
This surgeon had already taken Donal aside and
asked him if there were any marriage difficulties
that could be upsetting Nell. Donal racked his
brains and began to wonder if in fact Nell did have
problems of which he was not aware. They talked
together about it.

This atmosphere of doubt and uncertainty was
as much a trial to Nell as was the awful pain. Donal
left the baby in Dublin and went home to put in a
few days' work at the office. The other children
were still with Nell's sister. On New Year's evening
he was alone in the house waiting for a phone call
from the hospital.

When the surgeon called it was to tell him that
Nell had cancer and had about two years to live.
They had removed a tumour, which by reason of its
location was hidden and not discernible in X-ray.

Donal was deeply shocked and for a long time
he walked the kitchen floor, up and down, up and
down. Cancer had been ruled out from the very
beginning and it was the last thing he expected to
hear. Late evening and all as it was, he drove to
Dublin to his sister.

Next day he saw the surgeon, who advised him not to tell Nell the nature of her illness. He warned Donal that the next two years would be very difficult for them both, and that Nell would lean heavily on him for courage and support. The surgeon was obviously very upset.

And so began the harrowing task of covering up his misery and putting up a hopeful front for Nell. Donal's sister, who was a nun, at this time was a tower of strength. She, too, advised against telling Nell that she had cancer. Donal found that this particular sister had great strength of character. She supported him every inch of the way and encouraged him to hope that this two years could be a rewarding, even a happy experience.

Nell's mother and sister were also a great help and comfort. Donal never actually needed to tell Nell a lie about her condition. There had been an obstruction removed and she was perfectly satisfied that this indeed had been the cause of all her trouble. She also knew at this stage that another operation would be necessary when she had sufficiently regained her strength.

After her operation, with the pain no longer troubling her, Nell felt very much better. She was a good patient and even though her wound took a long time to heal she made the best of it. The surgeon, who before her operation had often seemed curt and impatient, was now most kind. Nell was determined to get better as fast as she could and when she came home she obeyed all the

instructions she had been given, even to drinking
Complan and laughing about it.

Donal remembers one evening she wheeled
Monica down town in her pram. This was quite an
achievement, and soon afterwards she went back to
Dublin for the second operation. For Donal this
meant the problem of another seven weeks keeping
the household organised. The woman who used to
help Nell twice a week began to come every day,
from 9.30 till 5.30. She was a good kind woman
and the children were very fond of her. Donal
would come home from work about 5.30, leave the
housekeeper to her own home, come back and get
supper, help with the lessons and get the children to
bed. Nell and he had discussed the question of
keeping the children together in their own home.
They felt it was better that they should feel
needed in the emergency of their mother's absence
and be fully aware that they were doing their bit to
help Daddy, and to support him until Mammy
would be well again. Apart from the Christmas
when Nell had her first operation, the children
were not sent away.

When Nell did come home there was another
good spell. She was very conscious of the children's
deprivation during her absence and was all set to
make it up to them in every way she could. One
thing she was determined to do was buy her older
daughter the prettiest dress she could get in the
town. Donal went with them, and together they
bought the daintiest dress of pale primrose with
short puff sleeves and a flared skirt that flowed

softly about the child with every step she took.

During this time Donal was kept so busy that he actually remembers feeling happy. He never quite gave up hope that Nell might recover. In this time, too, Nell and he drew ever closer and closer. Sometimes she would get depressed and tired and he would hold her in his arms and try to jolly her out of her gloom. Her back often ached and he became expert at knowing how to help her by massaging the trouble-spots. Donal said, "Sure come on now upstairs and we'll have a cuddle." Nell burst into tears and Donal felt something of her desperate frustrations.

Always bearing in mind his sister's advice, Donal made an effort to take Nell out somewhere special. They went to a few plays together and this they enjoyed very much.

Neighbours were a constant support. The community of nuns where his sister was offered continuous prayers for Nell and himself and the children. Donal says they were not over religious people, but he had a very definite feeling of being borne along by others' prayers and sympathy. Instead of the surgeon's two years, it transpired that there were only ten months left for Donal and Nell to be together.

A bout of pneumonia meant that Nell was taken to a local hospital, and before she left the house she was anointed. Even at that stage she would often talk about "When I get better" we'll do such-and-such a thing. There were other days when it would be "when I die".

While Nell was in hospital their older daughter broke her arm and had to be brought to the same hospital for X-ray and setting. Donal brought her in to see her Mammy, and the child (who was now almost seven) was immediately aware of the change in her mother's appearance. She had become very thin and her hair was arranged away from her face, so that she did not look like herself. When they came home the child asked her Daddy "Is Mammy going to die?" She cried bitterly and Donal felt that the child had, in that moment, seen that her mother was not going to get better. He did his best to comfort her.

Recovering after the pneumonia Nell asked was she going to die. At this stage Donal's sister felt she ought to be told, but thought he was the person to do it. And so he answered "Look, love, you nearly died last week and you pulled out of it. I'm hoping you will get better."

Nell's courage was a great help. She put a good face on things and was out doing her physiotherapy the day before she died. Her end was quiet and peaceful and she suffered no distressing pain.

Again Donal felt the support of his family. His sister and two of Nell's sisters stayed with him for two weeks. Having the aunts in the house was a help and there were many callers, so these weeks passed quickly.

The little girl who had seen her Mammy in hospital was very upset in a quiet way. She would not leave her Daddy's side. The boy of about nine was very emotional and cried a lot, but eventually shook it off much quicker than the little girl. It took her about a year to regain her confidence.

Donal, when the house had settled down, came to terms with awful loneliness. The first night after the aunts went away he put the children to bed, and came downstairs to an empty sitting-room. He sat down at the piano and found he was playing Nell's favourite tunes. He cried.

Evenings were terribly lonely. From the time work was finished and he got the housekeeper home, prepared tea, helped with the lessons and got the children to bed, he was very busy. He was always glad to have everyone settled down for the night, but his plight seemed to stare back at him from the empty sitting-room.

He admits that Nell's death was, in some ways, a relief. She had been so brave against so many odds that it was heartbreaking to watch her. She was not going to get better, and death brought an end to her suffering.

Donal says he couldn't imagine how anyone who had no faith would survive the sickness and death of a loving partner. He felt there must be some Divine purpose in such afflictions, and that no one has any particular right to stay alive anyway. He never questioned why Nell had to die, but he believed good would come from her death, both for her, for him and for the children. When the doctors had discovered the tumour after so many months of insisting that there was no reason for Nell's pain, he did not blame them. They had sought diligently for the cause and when they did not find it, he felt they had done their best, and it just simply was not to be that she was to be saved.

Beside this acceptance of God's purpose, he had always hoped there might be a reprieve. Donal recalls one evening he was visiting Nell in hospital, when the Dublin bomb victims were brought in. He was immediately grateful to God that Nell's illness was taking a quiet course, that he was sitting there beside her and that no mindless cruelty had deprived her of limbs or killed her. The desolation of those people's bitterness against the bombers made a deep impression on him. They were, he felt, doubly bereft.

Another thing that brought Donal relief after Nell's death was the fact that he could be open with the children about their Mammy's sickness. He had never been able to confide in them fully, in case their distress would be communicated to Nell. Now they talked together a lot about Mammy. They helped him in the house and together they chose a headstone for the grave. He went back on instances where they had asked him a particular question and he had been unable to answer it. Now everything was out in the open and he encouraged them to talk to him. "But you never know what goes on in a child's mind," says Donal. He hopes they have no problems now and he is fairly confident that they are coping.

Of course there are off days when he shouts at them, but this quickly blows over. Sunday mornings, getting everyone out to Mass is a scramble. Donal

says his own mother used to be cranky on Sunday
mornings before Mass. "Like a ferret" was the way
he described it. Now he, too, knows the tension of
getting boys to polish their shoes and getting the
older girl to brush her hair. The hair brushing
often brings tantrums and one Sunday morning he
got mad and threw the brush on the floor and
broke it. The child was feeling grumpy anyway,
she is the one who finds it hardest to get up in
the morning.

The boys cook breakfast, and Sunday dinner is
always a good meal. Donal goes to some trouble
to have roast beef and gravy or an Irish stew. He is
used to doing these things from his family experience and coping during Nell's illness.

The household was well organised and the
housekeeper a familiar, loving part of the children's lives. All in all the continuity he and Nell
had worked so hard to preserve during the many
hospital periods, now stood them all in good
stead.

Donal did not brood. Sometimes a neighbour
would take the children in after school with her
own children, help them with the lessons, give
them their tea and bring them home at bed-time. A
teenage girl from the neighbourhood was often a
baby-sitter. Now he feels his older son is able to
manage on his own. In the beginning, after he had
put the children to bed, he was encouraged by
neighbours to keep up his bridge. The bridge venue
is not far away and he always leaves a phone
number. He plays twice a week.

There was a funny incident once about a phone call. Donal had to go to work one morning at seven a.m. because there was a crisis on the job. He left the children his office number to ring in case of emergency. Just as he was getting down to dealing with a very knotty problem the phone rang. It was from home and this crying voice came across: "Daddy, Joe is after eating the last of the marmalade." "Well," said Daddy, "is there any jam?" "Yes," wailed the child. "Then eat that," said Daddy, and got back to his problem. Soon after came another call: "Daddy, Joe took all the cornflakes!" This time Donal told the child not to ring again unless someone was bleeding.

Apart from the sort of faith Donal has in God, he has learned the inestimable value of friendship. People have simply overwhelmed him with generosity and kindness. Nell's illness and the subsequent expensive domestic arrangements were a severe drain on his financial resources, but he decided that there was no point in trying to sort out these problems while there was so much else to cope with. After Nell's death when he began to sort out the bills, he found that members of his family or hers had already quietly settled these accounts. He had anticipated a certain amount of debt, but to his amazement this has not materialised.

Outside the family circle there was the devotion of the housekeeper and the encouragement of friends and neighbours. People whom he had dismissed as shallow socialisers he discovered to be concerned, and prepared to put themselves out to help him and the children.

Night prayers with the children is Donal's principal prayer period. They have never considered it necessary to pray for Nell's soul. He is quite convinced she is in heaven and would be more inclined to ask her help in an intercessory way, than pray for her release from purgatory. An annual Mass is regarded as a commemoration of Mammy, rather than a Mass offered for her soul. Donal accepts that people who die may not be prepared for a full understanding of heaven, but he does not see this as a period of expiation. He always had strong views about indulgences and prayers for the dead.

Donal has, so far, survived many trials and even though the nearest he could come to expressing the most harrowing experiences was "Ah, God, it was tough!" there is a joy and a hope in his household that reflects in the sparkling eyes of little Monica, in the open, uninhibited chatter of the older children and perhaps mostly in his own cheerful, relaxed maturity.

8 Myself: three years later

In early widowhood I felt quite barren. It reminded me of a black stunted tree I once saw. It was ugly in its bareness, stark in outline, with neither leaves nor swaying branches to lend it grace. It looked so lonely.

After three years of widowhood there are still things I find very hard — like coming into the house alone. My husband was a man who never felt the cold. I was seldom warm. In winter-time when we came into the house after Mass, the first thing he did was to put his arms around me and hold me until I was warm. Then he would start cooking the breakfast. On the rare occasions when I was out in the afternoon and he was in the house, he would have a lovely fire in the grate and my rocking chair pulled up waiting for me. Even now when I am going to bed at night there is so much of his care for me in the electric blanket, the reading lamp and the wall heater, that I talk to him and thank him for his goodness. He never read in bed. Nor did I while he was alive. Now I read for hours.

Immediately after my husband's death was a time of action. I changed the furniture round, sorted his clothes and gave them away, all except his favourite cap which still hangs in the hall. People were calling for quite a while. It was towards the end of summer and the two younger children were going back to school. There were two starting in jobs and coming home each evening, two others away at training schools and coming home at holiday time, and one working away from home and coming home at weekends.

Having the family meant there were meals to be cooked and the household just continued to run as it had always done. At first I used to feel that the children had very soon forgotten their father. Later I realised that they didn't talk about him because of me.

Looking back now I think the beginning was just an automatic continuance of the routine of the house. For a year and a half I had bad dreams and was greatly troubled. The dreams were never happy and I would wake up feeling upset and anxious. It almost seemed as if my husband was haunting me and I couldn't shake off this feeling of his disapproval and displeasure. Eventually I mentioned this to my doctor, who advised me to discontinue a sleeping tablet I had been taking. At no time had I taken tranquillisers. I felt this would only postpone facing up to the miseries I would eventually have to endure.

There are still times when my husband seems so near that I imagine I hear his car driving round by the gable of the house. I have found myself listening for the latch to lift on the back door. Had he walked in the door, I would not have been totally surprised.

Snatches of song, meeting old friends of his, seeing a man coming towards me in the street wearing a cap set at a rakish tilt, can set my heart racing.

Often I look around the kitchen table at teatime. I am glad that the children are coming home, that they go out together, that their friends come and go. When my little girl comes into my room at night, I know she feels safe because I am there.

Always I have disliked housework, but cannot live in squalor, so the cleaning, washing and cooking must be done. I prepare meals and clear up, only to start again. Sometimes I rebel inside myself. Whatever joy there was in housekeeping has gone. The boys don't seem to notice things like the garage door hanging off, the drains getting blocked, the damp patches on the wallpaper. I resort to nagging. I know that if my husband was here these chores would be done. Indeed these things would not happen at all. He would have seen the problems and dealt with them. Lately I had the crumbling kitchen walls plastered. We had no heat in the kitchen and no hot water. There was a lot of cleaning and scrubbing to be done. There was a problem about the chimney, and weeks passed before we got the heat back. I regretted ever having started. Now, thank God, it is done and I feel I may have started to shake off my lethargy.

Like every other widowed person, I think a lot

about the next life. I just cannot imagine what sort of life my husband now has. I cannot fit myself into his situation. I wonder have I any place in it at all. I grasp at any comforting thoughts I hear or read, like Charles Peguy's "Husband and wife will be in eternity like two hands uplifted in an unending adoration." Many saints, theologians and writers console us with their visions of happy reunions, but I still have not felt sure about any of this.

Someone writing to me after my husband's death reminded me that he had gone to God, and as God is always near so too was my husband. This has been my most consoling thought. I know that I talk to God a great deal of the time as I go about the house, or on the roads, or while I am awake at night. God turns into Felix. If I am not talking to God, I am talking to Felix.

For long spells I seem to be paralysed by laziness. I cannot tackle the everyday chores. I can look at a piece of wallpaper hanging off and I know I should mix a bit of paste and stick it on. But I do nothing.

Since I was sixteen years old I have gone to morning Mass and Holy Communion. For the past few months I have not gone to daily Mass. I drag myself out of bed in the morning to get my child to school. I sometimes go to bed in the afternoon, and yet I am tired. At least so I tell myself.

Looking back now it seems to me that I have been very fortunate in many ways. When I was two years widowed I attended a directed retreat.

Arrangements for the retreat were made by a friend of mine who had been greatly helped by this kind of exercise. I was most apprehensive about the idea of spending a few days in solitude. I went to that Retreat House planning to leave next day if I could not cope, and indeed I was almost certain that this kind of person-to-person arrangement would not work. I knew I was confused and drifting into a sort of helpless way of life. I had worries I felt quite incapable of sorting out. I felt as if life was stretching out ahead of me like a wasteland, a succession of days and nights.

The first evening I was there the Director came to talk to me. During that conversation I doggedly tried to describe my emptiness and tried to find words to express the nothingness that was in me. I knew I had come to the end of a part of my life, and I knew too that my grief could become a kind of self-pity. I felt I had to confront my own emptiness and accept the fact that life goes on. I didn't really expect the retreat to change anything. The priest listened and then suggested some reading I might do next day. He quoted a line from the Psalms. "Be still and know that I am God."

These words sort of blinded me, like as if a powerful searchlight had been focused on my soul. I felt as if God had brought me specially there to hear those words and they have helped me ever since in a most remarkable way. Whenever I am upset or worried I repeat them over and over until their meaning and depth sink into my soul. What was emptiness before, is now stillness. It's like

watching stones thrown into a deep well, making a
big noisy splash at the top but finally drifting softly
down to rest at the bottom. I will always be grateful to the friend who made that retreat possible.

Friends are so precious that I cannot describe
what they have meant to me. Other widows, who
know the loneliness and misery, are especially
close. No one who has not had the experience can
imagine the depths of suffering. The first bitter
sorrow heals with time but there are so many re-
finements of the torment of widowhood, that at
times we must appear neurotic, selfish, even
slightly insane.

As a woman who continues to be a full-time
housewife, there are times when depression simply
sits down on top of me. Sometimes I have been
rescued by a friend pushing in the kitchen door
and stopping for a chat. Sometimes by a letter or
phone call. There have been the times when I've
settled myself down to do the ironing with a
glass of sherry on the draining board. I know there
is danger here. I think I must be careful not to have
two. If I were rich enough to keep a supply of
drink in the house, I think I might drink too much.
So far I've managed all right. A glass of sherry
before tea seems like a break at the end of the day.
It's almost like someone coming in when the day's
work is over. After tea I have no problem. There
are lessons, a fire to sit by, the newspaper to read
or some piece of needlework to do. I hate mending
or darning. I like to make something and watch it
grow. Then there is the pleasure of reading in

bed. I read for hours. Indeed, books have been a tremendous help.

Regrets are always cropping up. I think about my husband sleeping downstairs when he had his leg amputated, while all the rest of us went upstairs to bed. I often wonder if he ever woke at night and felt lonely. I should have arranged that the boys would sleep downstairs in turn.   I feel I was often unsympathetic. When I think now of my man's frustrations, I know he must have suffered a great deal more than pain and discomfort. He must have known he was not getting stronger. He must have realised he might not make it and might have to leave us. He had such tremendous foresight and such qualities of organisation that he must have worried about me. At times my quiet pace must have exasperated him. He would have known that we would have problems running the house without his salary when some of the children were still at school and others just starting work.

All I am quite sure about is the love he knew I had for him in spite of my inability to measure up to his standards of organisation. He knew I would always look after him and he actually prayed that God would leave me my health long enough to nurse him back to a normal life. During our marriage I had often been sick. He, seldom. God answered his prayer.

Another regret I now have is that I had not asserted myself early on in our marriage. As far as my husband was concerned he was the boss, and I was happy this way. But as the children

grew older he found it hard to accept their adult-
hood. He just continued to organise them as if
they were school children. This, of courses,
created tensions. I blame myself entirely for this
now.

The children were aware that their father's
illness demanded their patience and consideration.
They tried not to annoy him. I think they learned
a lot from this situation. I notice whenever occasions arise now when their father would have acted
in a particular way, they act much the same as he
would. They would object to any watering down
on discipline where the younger ones are concerned. They are involving themselves in the
home situations that arise, other than manual
work. At Christmas they decide among themselves as to who buy what. One supplies the turkey,
one the ham and one the wine and cidona we
drink on Christmas Day.

Festive seasons, holidays and weekends are a
nightmare. Always on Sunday afternoons we used
to go for a drive and a walk. Now I go to bed and
close the curtains. Often I have shut out the
bright summer sunshine and the sound of children
playing. I would get up more miserable than ever.
Lately I have been trying to resume the walking
pattern. Sometimes I go alone. Sometimes my
little girl comes with me. I love Sunday evening
devotions in the church. It helps me to close one
week and start another. Choir work and music
have been helpful because they have required my

concentration on something outside the home
and demand my full attention.

Writing imposes the same sort of discipline.
For many years I have kept a journal, but it has
dropped out of my programme. My 1976 diary
shows little but accounts and appointments.
Otherwise, blank pages.

There is great consolation for me in the continuing unity of the family. We talk things over.
The children's differing personalities bring con-
flicting views, but so far they have accepted whatever decisions I have made.

A great tradition in our house had been good
food. My husband would come home laden with
meat, fresh fruit and always a gift each for the
younger children. I, too, would get a delicacy in
season, like peaches or fresh salmon. All that is
gone from our lives now. Our fridge is often bare,
where once it was crammed. But we still have
enough to eat, thank God. My sons often come
home with a bag of potatoes or a piece of bacon—
just like their father used to do.

Children undoubtedly are a great help. They
bring worries and responsibilities perhaps, but
basically they are a support, a reason for living.

Maybe this is one of the hardest things to bear,
not having one person at the centre of your life.
The children have their own lives and interests.

One day in particular I remember coming
home from hospital. My son had collected me and
we arrived about lunch time. The children had
a day off school for the funeral of President

Childers. They were all around the kitchen watching television. When they had taken their eyes off television long enough to say welcome home, they turned their attention back to it. The kitchen was untidy. There was a heap of dirty clothes for washing. I felt abandoned.

More than anything else I miss this feeling of belonging to the one very special person. There's not much thrill now in dressing up or trying to look well. I miss the sparkle of appreciation in my husband's eyes.

I long for him, to feel his hands, to hear his voice. Other interests are merely substitute. Middle age is dreary with its wrinkles, slackening muscles and greying hair. When I look in the mirror and see this dull-eyed, ageing woman, I close my eyes to shut out the sight. Love makes its own sparkle. Tenderness softens a woman's face.

Love has been a very precious gift, which I think I have never properly valued. There are times when I am overwhelmed by the implications of our love. At Christmas-time, when our daughter lights the Christmas candle in the window, it brings me back twenty-seven years to the first Christmas we were married and my husband lit the candle and set it in the window. It's as if he lit the way that night for me and the children. Nothing really ends after all.

Accepting the fact that my husband is not with us any more, I am also beginning to accept that life goes on. The children are growing and they expect my support. They take a loving home for granted, they always had it. They seem to have survived the deprivation of a good and generous father. They accept my inadequacies and in different ways have supported me.

I thank God for them and as I constantly pray for them all and commend them to God's loving care, I have confidence in their future. I feel always that God is the centre of love. There I meet my husband and in my prayers bring myself and the family. I know we are all together then, and I feel secure. Sometimes even happy.